McGraw-Hill Education

500

MAT

Questions

to know by test day

McGraw-Hill Education

500
MAT
Questions

to know by test day

Kathy A. Zahler, MS

New York Chicago San Francisco Athens London Madrid
Mexico City Milan New Delhi Singapore Sydney Toronto

1 2 3 4 5 6 7 8 9 10   QFR/QFR   1 0 9 8 7 6 5 4

ISBN   978-0-07-183210-6
MHID   0-07-183210-6

e-ISBN   978-0-07-183211-3
e-MHID   0-07-183211-4

Library of Congress Control Number 2014934946

The Miller Analogies Test (MAT) is a registered trademark of NCS Pearson, Inc.,
which was not involved in the production of, and does not endorse, this
product.

McGraw-Hill Education products are available at special quantity discounts to
use as premiums and sales promotions or for use in corporate training programs.
To contact a representative, please visit the Contact Us pages at
www.mhprofessional.com.

This book is printed on acid-free paper.

CONTENTS

INTRODUCTION

Congratulations! You've taken a big step toward success on the Miller Analogies Test by purchasing *McGraw-Hill Education: 500 MAT Questions to Know by Test Day*. We are here to help you take the next step and score high on your MAT exam so you can get into the graduate school of your choice!

This book gives you 500 MAT-style, multiple-choice questions that encompass the 10 main types of relationships and the key concepts and disciplines covered by the MAT. Each question is clearly explained in the answer key. The questions will give you valuable independent practice to supplement your earlier review.

This book and the others in the series were written by expert teachers who know the subject inside and out and can identify crucial information as well as the kinds of questions that are most likely to appear on the exam.

You might be the kind of student who needs to study extra a few weeks before the exam for a final review. Or you might be the kind of student who puts off preparing until the last minute before the exam. No matter what your preparation style, you will benefit from reviewing these 500 questions, which closely parallel the content, format, and degree of difficulty of the questions on the actual MAT exam. These questions and the explanations in the answer key are the ideal, last-minute study tool for those final weeks before the test.

If you practice with all the questions and answers in this book, we are certain that you will build the skills and confidence needed to excel on the MAT. Good luck!

—Editors of McGraw-Hill Education

McGraw-Hill Education

500
MAT
Questions

to know by test day

CHAPTER 1

Synonym Analogies

In this type of analogy, if the correspondence is A is to B as C is to D, and A and B are synonyms, then C and D are synonyms. If the correspondence is A is to C as B is to D, and A and C are synonyms, then B and D are synonyms.

1. DAMAGED : SPOILED :: FIXED : _____
   - (A) detached
   - (B) refurbished
   - (C) razed
   - (D) varied

2. CANDOR : _____ :: DANDER : TEMPER
   - (A) insincerity
   - (B) ruse
   - (C) compassion
   - (D) frankness

3. HUMBLE : HUMBUG :: _____ : IMPOSTER
   - (A) fumble
   - (B) arrogant
   - (C) modest
   - (D) poster

4. FRUSTRATED : THWARTED :: TAINTED : _____

    (A) uninvolved
    (B) dyed
    (C) enriched
    (D) fouled

5. _____ : BOOST :: THRASH : UPLIFT

    (A) pummel
    (B) elevate
    (C) deride
    (D) muddle

6. HAZE : CLOUDBURST :: MIASMA : _____

    (A) downpour
    (B) smog
    (C) tempest
    (D) cyclone

7. _____ : REVOLVE :: DIVE : PLUMMET

    (A) evolve
    (B) surround
    (C) rotate
    (D) alternate

8. CAESURA : PAUSE :: _____ : REPETITION

    (A) metonymy
    (B) elision
    (C) anaphora
    (D) apostrophe

9. FIXATIVE : _____ :: ADHESIVE : LACQUER
   (A) surface
   (B) adherent
   (C) varnish
   (D) denture

10. _____ : GUFFAW :: DRONE : CHANT
    (A) chortle
    (B) attack
    (C) vocalize
    (D) squawk

11. FABRICATED : CONSTRUCTED :: DOUSED : _____
    (A) assembled
    (B) decorated
    (C) augmented
    (D) immersed

12. PRIOR : _____ :: NEVERTHELESS : YET
    (A) behindhand
    (B) subsequently
    (C) however
    (D) heretofore

13. EXONERATE : EXORCISE :: _____ : EXPEL
    (A) execrate
    (B) absolve
    (C) excommunicate
    (D) impel

14. _____ : ELUCIDATE :: POLLUTE : ADULTERATE

    (A) progress

    (B) defile

    (C) ignite

    (D) clarify

15. RADIANCE : DEXTERITY :: _____ : AGILITY

    (A) spryness

    (B) luminosity

    (C) tedium

    (D) calumny

16. _____ : SACRILEGE :: REVERENCE : VENERATION

    (A) worship

    (B) heresy

    (C) penance

    (D) devotion

17. FAUX PAS : GAFFE :: IDÉE FIXE : _____

    (A) correction

    (B) delight

    (C) brainstorm

    (D) obsession

18. ROUTINELY : _____ :: DESPITE : NOTWITHSTANDING

    (A) customarily

    (B) dully

    (C) although

    (D) curiously

19. PLEDGE : VOUCHSAFE :: DECRY : _____

   (A) condemn

   (B) guarantee

   (C) snivel

   (D) commend

20. _____ : SUAVE :: VALIANT : BRAVE

   (A) debonair

   (B) noble

   (C) clever

   (D) naive

21. IV : 4 :: _____ : 14

   (A) VI

   (B) XIIII

   (C) XIV

   (D) XVI

22. POLEMIC : POSTULATE :: DIATRIBE : _____

   (A) review

   (B) verdict

   (C) assertion

   (D) antagonism

23. EXTRAVAGANT : _____ :: RAVENOUS : VORACIOUS

   (A) widespread

   (B) profligate

   (C) substantial

   (D) insatiable

24. _____ : TARN :: BOND : POND

  (A) auction
  (B) pool
  (C) trinket
  (D) rapport

25. GAMUT : RANGE :: GAMIN : _____

  (A) humbug
  (B) victory
  (C) neighborhood
  (D) urchin

26. UBIQUITOUS : _____ :: OMNIPRESENT : OMNIPOTENT

  (A) universal
  (B) effective
  (C) almighty
  (D) servile

27. REPARATION : COMPENSATION :: SEPARATION : _____

  (A) remuneration
  (B) amalgamation
  (C) condensation
  (D) partition

28. _____ : RECANT :: RECTIFY : REDRESS

  (A) depose
  (B) dismiss
  (C) disavow
  (D) declaim

29. ONEROUS : BURDENSOME :: PERSPICACIOUS : _____

    (A) tactful

    (B) insightful

    (C) robust

    (D) taxing

30. DISHONOR : _____ :: STIGMA : ENIGMA

    (A) puzzle

    (B) doctrine

    (C) element

    (D) discredit

31. GROUNDHOG : WOODCHUCK :: _____ : POLECAT

    (A) bobcat

    (B) raccoon

    (C) skunk

    (D) cougar

32. RETICENT : RETICULE :: RESERVED : _____

    (A) shyness

    (B) superstition

    (C) purse

    (D) compost

33. RISIBLE : _____ :: VISIBLE : EVIDENT

    (A) uplifting

    (B) obvious

    (C) ludicrous

    (D) heartwarming

34. À LA MODE : TRENDY :: AVANT GARDE : _____

   (A) innovative
   (B) confrontational
   (C) productive
   (D) outmoded

35. SUPERSEDE : EXCEED :: _____ : OUTDO

   (A) overdo
   (B) reorder
   (C) supplant
   (D) re-create

36. CONNECTION : CORRELATION :: _____ : SCHISM

   (A) granite
   (B) division
   (C) bond
   (D) vacuum

37. FOURTH ESTATE : PRESS :: FIFTH COLUMN : _____

   (A) poor
   (B) upper classes
   (C) subversives
   (D) plebes

38. IMPETUS : _____ :: INERTIA : INACTION

   (A) torpor
   (B) rashness
   (C) value
   (D) momentum

39. _____ : VEER :: GAZE : PEER

    (A) yaw

    (B) linger

    (C) gape

    (D) guide

40. BELEAGUER : FACILITATE :: _____ : ENABLE

    (A) gratify

    (B) alter

    (C) empower

    (D) harass

41. _____ : TEMBLOR :: INFERNO : EARTHQUAKE

    (A) paradise

    (B) conflagration

    (C) seism

    (D) shock

42. WORRISOME : _____ :: SUSPICIOUS : DUBIOUS

    (A) disquieting

    (B) ambiguous

    (C) enlightening

    (D) noteworthy

43. _____ : AT PLEASURE :: AD INFINITUM : TO INFINITY

    (A) ad hominem

    (B) ad libitum

    (C) ad interim

    (D) ad valorem

44. FRAUDULENT : FLAVORFUL :: COUNTERFEIT : _____
- (A) faux
- (B) currency
- (C) savory
- (D) featureless

45. ARROYO : GULCH :: _____ : ISLAND
- (A) canyon
- (B) canal
- (C) key
- (D) cove

46. GELID : FROZEN :: PLIABLE : _____
- (A) constructive
- (B) slender
- (C) elastic
- (D) polar

47. _____ : WHIP :: TRUNCHEON : CROP
- (A) cudgel
- (B) spike
- (C) lash
- (D) projectile

48. BLAMEWORTHY : REPREHENSIBLE :: PLAUSIBLE : _____
- (A) culpable
- (B) logical
- (C) oracular
- (D) influential

49. VIOLENT : AGGRESSIVE :: _____ : SUBMISSIVE

   (A) brutal

   (B) passive

   (C) packaged

   (D) inferential

50. _____ : SONOROUS :: STRIDENT : SHRILL

   (A) resonant

   (B) clamorous

   (C) agreeable

   (D) reedy

CHAPTER 2

Antonym Analogies

In this type of analogy, if the correspondence is A is to B as C is to D, and A and B are antonyms, then C and D are antonyms. If the correspondence is A is to C as B is to D, and A and C are antonyms, then B and D are antonyms.

51. DOTE : DOTAGE :: _____ : YOUTH

    (A) neglect

    (B) young

    (C) teenager

    (D) adore

52. ADULT : JUVENILE :: SHAM : _____

    (A) bogus

    (B) bona fide

    (C) sage

    (D) quack

53. HALE : _____ :: NEAT : DISORDERLY

    (A) muscular

    (B) ailing

    (C) chaotic

    (D) vigorous

54. SCHISM : UNION :: ENNUI : _____

    (A) eagerness

    (B) grievance

    (C) disorder

    (D) tedium

55. EFFUSIVE: _____ :: PROFICIENT : INCOMPETENT

    (A) weighty

    (B) feeble

    (C) insolent

    (D) reticent

56. BRASH : GENEROUS :: _____ : STINGY

    (A) casual

    (B) aggressive

    (C) inexpert

    (D) restrained

57. FRANTIC : UNRUFFLED :: BEWILDERED : _____

    (A) confused

    (B) enlightened

    (C) ruffled

    (D) stupefied

58. FEVERISH : CHILLY :: _____ : SLUGGISH

    (A) slow

    (B) ill

    (C) frigid

    (D) animated

59. SOAR : SOUR :: _____ : SUGARY

    (A) plummet
    (B) extend
    (C) pressure
    (D) indulge

60. EQUANIMITY : VOLATILITY :: IMMOBILITY : _____

    (A) disorientation
    (B) illumination
    (C) motion
    (D) unevenness

61. UNIFORM : INCONSISTENT :: _____ : AMBIGUOUS

    (A) unintended
    (B) obvious
    (C) constant
    (D) subtle

62. CACOPHONY : EUPHONY :: _____ : EUPHORIA

    (A) dissonance
    (B) cachet
    (C) despair
    (D) amphora

63. _____ : SAGE :: FIEND : SERAPH

    (A) herb
    (B) wisdom
    (C) fool
    (D) wizard

64. TREACHERY : CHIVALRY :: _____ : RUDENESS

(A) decorum
(B) betrayal
(C) insolence
(D) loyalty

65. _____ : AFICIONADO :: HAUTEUR : HATER

(A) humility
(B) astuteness
(C) design
(D) fan

66. ALTER : PRESERVE :: FALTER : _____

(A) persist
(B) abate
(C) amend
(D) protect

67. GAIN : LOSS :: _____ : OXIDATION

(A) reduction
(B) profit
(C) metabolism
(D) combustion

68. _____ : FACILE :: MALADROIT : AGILE

(A) slippery
(B) handmade
(C) awkward
(D) profound

69. INFIRMITY : WELL-BEING :: _____ : WELL-WISHER

- (A) ailment
- (B) disparager
- (C) neurotic
- (D) appraiser

70. _____ : VIOLET :: GREEN : RED

- (A) purple
- (B) blue
- (C) yellow
- (D) pink

71. EAST : _____ :: NORTHEAST : SOUTHWEST

- (A) northwest
- (B) north
- (C) southeast
- (D) west

72. UNMASK : RETREAT :: _____ : ADVANCE

- (A) moderate
- (B) reward
- (C) disguise
- (D) surmise

73. PIGHEADED : FISHY :: FLEXIBLE : _____

- (A) singed
- (B) inelastic
- (C) observant
- (D) above-board

74. _____ : DISCOURAGE :: DIMINISH : INTENSIFY

- (A) motivate
- (B) coerce
- (C) falsify
- (D) suppress

75. WRONGHEADED : ASTUTE :: PHLEGMATIC : _____

- (A) parched
- (B) healthy
- (C) incisive
- (D) energetic

76. _____ : UNCOMMON :: PREDICTABLE : UNEXPECTED

- (A) erratic
- (B) preponderant
- (C) exclusive
- (D) obvious

77. FORTUNATE : _____ :: REPUTABLE : INFAMOUS

- (A) providential
- (B) cataclysmic
- (C) notorious
- (D) surreptitious

78. WATERTIGHT : PERMEABLE :: MALLEABLE : _____

- (A) firm
- (B) vigorous
- (C) plausible
- (D) expressive

79. METTLE : MEDDLE :: _____ : IGNORE

   (A) cowardice

   (B) penalty

   (C) steel

   (D) surmise

80. _____ : JADED :: EXPERIENCED : GREEN

   (A) prompt

   (B) mature

   (C) babyish

   (D) enthusiastic

81. GRANDILOQUENT : _____ :: GRACEFUL : UNGAINLY

   (A) straightforward

   (B) clumsy

   (C) pompous

   (D) lissome

82. _____ : BEGINNING :: FINALE : PRELUDE

   (A) climax

   (B) denouement

   (C) structure

   (D) overture

83. JEJUNE : _____ :: METICULOUS : SLIPSHOD

   (A) candid

   (B) careless

   (C) pretentious

   (D) sophisticated

84. MUNDANE : SERVILE :: EXOTIC : _____

(A) foreign
(B) tenacious
(C) assertive
(D) dreary

85. _____ : OPPRESSIVE :: AUSPICIOUS : LENIENT

(A) frigid
(B) unlucky
(C) sensible
(D) tolerant

86. GARRULOUS : TACITURN :: ARTICULATE : _____

(A) expressive
(B) reticulate
(C) pacific
(D) incoherent

87. _____ : EVEN-TEMPERED :: UNFAIR : EVENHANDED

(A) noxious
(B) righteous
(C) fractious
(D) imperturbable

88. TENACIOUS : TENABLE :: IRRESOLUTE : _____

(A) firm
(B) dogged
(C) unsound
(D) unfastened

89. PEON : PATRICIAN :: _____ : NATIVE

- (A) soldier
- (B) alien
- (C) noble
- (D) operative

90. SUSPECT : DISSUADE :: TRUST : _____

- (A) encourage
- (B) presume
- (C) deter
- (D) ordain

91. SENSATION : NUMBNESS :: CONFLICT : _____

- (A) detachment
- (B) concord
- (C) gratification
- (D) variance

92. PERPETUAL : PROVISIONAL :: _____ : VOLUNTARY

- (A) charitable
- (B) compulsory
- (C) optional
- (D) regular

93. _____ : PUGNACIOUS :: MATURE : PEACEABLE

- (A) truculent
- (B) puerile
- (C) veteran
- (D) adamant

94. _____ : INNOCUOUS :: HOSTILE : CONGENIAL

    (A) inoffensive

    (B) affable

    (C) poisonous

    (D) unreceptive

95. TARNISHED : UNSULLIED :: BANISHED : _____

    (A) elated

    (B) rejuvenated

    (C) unfinished

    (D) accepted

96. SORORAL : _____ :: MATERNAL : PATERNAL

    (A) avuncular

    (B) crepuscular

    (C) ladylike

    (D) fraternal

97. SANGUINE : HOMOGENEOUS :: _____ : DISSIMILAR

    (A) pessimistic

    (B) undamaged

    (C) antiseptic

    (D) placid

98. TERMINATE : FOUND :: EXTERMINATE : _____

    (A) hearten

    (B) revive

    (C) expire

    (D) dictate

99. _____ : VENERABLE :: FALSE : DISREPUTABLE

    (A) revered
    (B) vanquished
    (C) veritable
    (D) inventive

100. REMARKABLE : MUNDANE :: FERAL : _____

    (A) humdrum
    (B) notable
    (C) domesticated
    (D) undaunted

CHAPTER **3**

Degree Analogies

Degree analogies are similar to synonym analogies, except that in a degree analogy, one word in each pair is greater in some way than the other, as in *big* and *humongous* or *trembling* and *shuddering*.

101. POLITE : OBSEQUIOUS :: LENIENT : _____

    (A) spineless

    (B) moderate

    (C) rude

    (D) strict

102. OBESE : CHUBBY :: _____ : DISRUPTIVE

    (A) uncontrollable

    (B) distracting

    (C) helpful

    (D) fretful

103. COLLAPSE : _____ :: REQUEST : IMPORTUNE

    (A) appeal

    (B) tumble

    (C) implode

    (D) subside

104. REPLICA : FORGERY :: CHAGRIN : _____

    (A) valor

    (B) candor

    (C) mortification

    (D) precision

105. THROW : _____ :: SIT : FLOP

    (A) hurl

    (B) spill

    (C) catch

    (D) hand

106. MANIC : BUSY :: _____ : NOISY

    (A) happy

    (B) deafening

    (C) industrious

    (D) silent

107. FEARFUL : TERRIFIED :: _____ : ASTOUNDED

    (A) petrified

    (B) surprised

    (C) miraculous

    (D) unconcerned

108. WANT : LIKE :: _____ : WORSHIP

    (A) need

    (B) venerate

    (C) crave

    (D) loathe

109. BOTTLE : MAGNUM :: PLATE : _____

    (A) spoon

    (B) flask

    (C) dish

    (D) salver

110. VERY : EXTREMELY :: _____ : RARELY

(A) intermittently

(B) frequently

(C) particularly

(D) finally

111. _____ : WILY :: DURABLE : INDESTRUCTIBLE

(A) ingenuous

(B) honest

(C) strong

(D) clever

112. KEEN : FANATICAL :: INTERESTED : _____

(A) engrossed

(B) indifferent

(C) sharp

(D) surprised

113. VIAL : VAT :: FILAMENT : _____

(A) hair

(B) tub

(C) strand

(D) rope

114. _____ : HARANGUE :: STORE : HOARD

(A) defeat

(B) lecture

(C) amass

(D) weep

115. MISCHIEVOUS : SELF-INDULGENT :: WICKED : _____

 (A) enthralled

 (B) nasty

 (C) confident

 (D) hedonistic

116. MELODY : ARIA :: _____ : PROM

 (A) tune

 (B) dance

 (C) feast

 (D) promenade

117. MISDEMEANOR : _____ :: PETIT LARCENY : GRAND LARCENY

 (A) theft

 (B) burglary

 (C) felony

 (D) crime

118. PUSH : PULL :: SHOVE : _____

 (A) force

 (B) cease

 (C) rope

 (D) yank

119. PROTECT : GUARD :: _____ : STOCKPILE

 (A) collect

 (B) admire

 (C) scrutinize

 (D) disclose

120. PROD : STAB :: DISOBEY : _____

    (A) wound

    (B) punish

    (C) flout

    (D) conform

121. _____ : SATURATE :: SENTIMENTAL : MAUDLIN

    (A) tinge

    (B) dehydrate

    (C) amuse

    (D) eliminate

122. IMAGINATION : CONCERN :: _____ : ANXIETY

    (A) delusion

    (B) sensation

    (C) interest

    (D) modernism

123. _____ : GRIM :: UNWIELDY : CUMBERSOME

    (A) sober

    (B) bulky

    (C) entertained

    (D) salubrious

124. STOMP : TREAD :: CLOBBER : _____

    (A) argue

    (B) strike

    (C) plod

    (D) differ

125. _____ : LIVID :: RESTLESS : FRANTIC

    (A) serene

    (B) disgruntled

    (C) restive

    (D) hysterical

126. FAD : MANIA :: ENJOYMENT : _____

    (A) impulse

    (B) crush

    (C) encouragement

    (D) enthrallment

127. WAVE : TSUNAMI :: HOLLOW : _____

    (A) hole

    (B) ripple

    (C) tani

    (D) chasm

128. GROUP : THRONG :: _____ : JUNGLE

    (A) woodland

    (B) leopard

    (C) humidity

    (D) cluster

129. SPEW : OUTLAW :: EMIT : _____

    (A) eject

    (B) ponder

    (C) permit

    (D) forbid

130. FOLLOW : DRIBBLE :: _____ : SLOBBER

(A) stalk

(B) lead

(C) bounce

(D) trickle

131. _____ : FEEBLE :: FIT : BRAWNY

(A) delicate

(B) incapacitated

(C) adequate

(D) stalwart

132. _____ : DOTING :: HARMFUL : DESTRUCTIVE

(A) damaging

(B) elderly

(C) fond

(D) uncaring

133. FULL : UNTIDY :: _____ : SLOVENLY

(A) void

(B) jumbled

(C) satisfied

(D) bursting

134. MELLOW : PLUMMY :: HIGH-PITCHED : _____

(A) alto

(B) noisy

(C) piercing

(D) wealthy

135. WATERFALL : _____ :: BLUFF : PRECIPICE

    (A) crag

    (B) outflow

    (C) spring

    (D) cataract

136. OPTIMISTIC : TRIUMPHANT :: LUKEWARM : _____

    (A) celebratory

    (B) keen

    (C) fluid

    (D) apathetic

137. ABRUPT : RUDE :: LONG : _____

    (A) coarse

    (B) brief

    (C) thin

    (D) protracted

138. APPROVE : BLESS :: DISAPPROVE : _____

    (A) repel

    (B) desecrate

    (C) disagree

    (D) censure

139. INFLUENCE : _____ :: CONNECT : BIND

    (A) unite

    (B) declare

    (C) impel

    (D) commit

140. HARMFUL : TOXIC :: _____ : HOSTILE

    (A) disapproving
    (B) dangerous
    (C) wasteful
    (D) troubling

141. _____ : INCONSEQUENTIAL :: NEEDY : DESTITUTE

    (A) minor
    (B) positive
    (C) deprived
    (D) ensuing

142. ACHIEVE : THRIVE :: _____ : AGONIZE

    (A) profit
    (B) scuffle
    (C) realize
    (D) worry

143. _____ : UNDEVIATING :: BRIEF : BRUSQUE

    (A) direct
    (B) unerring
    (C) offhand
    (D) sloppy

144. TAME : SUBJUGATE :: USE : _____

    (A) treat
    (B) squander
    (C) vanquish
    (D) tarnish

145. _____ : JUGGERNAUT :: MARCH : STAMPEDE

    (A) force

    (B) size

    (C) space

    (D) sloppy

146. SHACK : REPRESSION :: HOVEL : _____

    (A) hut

    (B) autonomy

    (C) suspect

    (D) slavery

147. ACCEDE : SURRENDER :: WANE : _____

    (A) yield

    (B) devour

    (C) disappear

    (D) wax

148. _____ : PARTICULAR :: PERVERTED : UNNATURAL

    (A) finicky

    (B) relaxed

    (C) atypical

    (D) evident

149. NEGLECT : _____ :: PESTER : HARASS

    (A) stalk

    (B) nurture

    (C) clamber

    (D) abandon

150. ARTERY : ARTERIOLE :: VEIN : _____

    (A) varicose

    (B) heart valve

    (C) venule

    (D) vena cava

CHAPTER 4

Affix Analogies

An affix is a word part. The MAT tests prefixes, suffixes, and roots and expects you to know what they mean or how they change a word.

151. -ER : _____ :: -FUL : FULL OF

    (A) most
    (B) again
    (C) not
    (D) one who

152. QUASI- : _____ :: HEMI- : HALF

    (A) quarter
    (B) somewhat
    (C) more
    (D) verified

153. _____ : AD- :: AWAY FROM : TOWARD

    (A) ab-
    (B) auto-
    (C) inter-
    (D) post-

154. MEGA- : _____ :: MACRO- : LARGE

    (A) not
    (B) loud
    (C) beyond
    (D) huge

155. XER : XYL :: DRY : _____

    (A) damp

    (B) foreign

    (C) wooden

    (D) heavy

156. VERB : VERT :: WORD : _____

    (A) turn

    (B) tree

    (C) stop

    (D) color

157. OMNI- : _____ :: ALL : MANY

    (A) poly-

    (B) ambi-

    (C) meta-

    (D) ante-

158. KILO- : _____ :: THOUSAND : HUNDRED

    (A) milli-

    (B) hecto-

    (C) deci-

    (D) multi-

159. POLI : CITY :: PERI : _____

    (A) false

    (B) cold

    (C) local

    (D) around

160. _____ : FAITH :: MORT : DEATH

(A) fid

(B) mut

(C) nav

(D) lex

161. CEREBRO : BRAIN :: CRANIO : _____

(A) bone

(B) skull

(C) liver

(D) sense

162. _____ : EQUAL :: ETHNO- : PEOPLE

(A) arch-

(B) epi-

(C) uni-

(D) iso-

163. -IST : _____ :: NOUN : ADJECTIVE

(A) -ism

(B) -ing

(C) -ish

(D) -ite

164. _____ : WHITE :: LACTO : LEUKO

(A) milk

(B) silver

(C) sugar

(D) side

165. SECT : SPECT :: TO CUT : _____

    (A) to reveal

    (B) to place

    (C) to write

    (D) to look

166. TELO- : _____ :: TELE- : DISTANT

    (A) far

    (B) end

    (C) earth

    (D) prior

167. OCTA : _____ :: 8 : 12

    (A) deca

    (B) ennea

    (C) dodeca

    (D) binal

168. HYPO : BELOW :: HOMO : _____

    (A) atop

    (B) same

    (C) without

    (D) unlike

169. MIS- : _____ :: IM- : NOT

    (A) hardly

    (B) at

    (C) nothing

    (D) wrong

170. DICT : DUCT :: TO SPEAK : _____

   (A) to lead
   (B) to fall
   (C) to listen
   (D) to show

171. SUPER- : _____ :: ABOVE : ACROSS

   (A) supra-
   (B) fore-
   (C) inter-
   (D) trans-

172. CHRON : DYNA :: TIME : _____

   (A) sound
   (B) luck
   (C) power
   (D) life

173. HATE : LOVE :: _____ : PHILO

   (A) miso
   (B) nym
   (C) phobia
   (D) tele

174. -ITY : _____ :: -FUL : FULL OF

   (A) state of
   (B) one who
   (C) can be
   (D) without

175. MICRO- : MILLIONTH :: NANO- : _____

    (A) thousandth
    (B) ten-thousandth
    (C) ten-millionth
    (D) billionth

176. BOTH : MANY :: _____ : MULTI

    (A) bene
    (B) ambi
    (C) vidi
    (D) alti

177. AROUND : _____ :: CIRCUM : CONTRA

    (A) against
    (B) within
    (C) alike
    (D) unless

178. TRI- : THREE :: SEPT- : _____

    (A) four
    (B) six
    (C) seven
    (D) nine

179. FRAG : BREAK :: _____ : FLOW

    (A) hyper
    (B) flux
    (C) pend
    (D) struct

180. ACRI : AGRI :: SOUR : _____

   (A) field

   (B) fight

   (C) activity

   (D) sweet

181. ULTRA- : ULTIMA- :: EXTREMELY : _____

   (A) last

   (B) approximately

   (C) outside

   (D) made of

182. FOUR : NINE :: TETRA : _____

   (A) hexa

   (B) deka

   (C) ennea

   (D) pente

183. _____ : COUNTER :: WITH : AGAINST

   (A) com

   (B) corp

   (C) circum

   (D) centri

184. FOOT : _____ :: PED : PEDO

   (A) leg

   (B) age

   (C) child

   (D) drive

185. _____ : NAME :: NEUR : NOM

    (A) new

    (B) nerve

    (C) birth

    (D) inside

186. INFRA : INTRA :: _____ : WITHIN

    (A) beneath

    (B) instead

    (C) without

    (D) over

187. PHLEGMA : PNEUMA :: INFLAMMATION : _____

    (A) breath

    (B) bruise

    (C) tears

    (D) wheel

188. PHAGE : _____ :: RUPT : BREAK

    (A) show

    (B) create

    (C) eat

    (D) fix

189. VERI : TRUE :: VITA : _____

    (A) false

    (B) strong

    (C) old

    (D) alive

190. _____ : VERB :: -LY : ADVERB

    (A) -able

    (B) -ize

    (C) -ment

    (D) -ful

191. DEXTRO- : _____ :: RIGHT : LEFT

(A) dorso-
(B) facio-
(C) idio-
(D) sinistro-

192. GASTRO- : HEPATO- :: STOMACH : _____

(A) blood
(B) lung
(C) cell
(D) liver

193. -LEPSY : -LYSIS :: ATTACK : _____

(A) falling
(B) destruction
(C) gathering
(D) connection

194. GRESS : GRAPH :: _____ : TO WRITE

(A) to form
(B) to sing
(C) to walk
(D) to decline

195. LIPO- : _____ :: LITHO- : STONE

(A) light
(B) fat
(C) smooth
(D) lateral

196. VAC : VOC :: _____ : CALL

(A) strong
(B) empty
(C) unified
(D) free

197. SUN : _____ :: LIGHT : LUM

    (A) sume

    (B) terra

    (C) helio

    (D) annu

198. HEMO- : HEMI- :: _____ : HALF

    (A) deficient

    (B) sleep

    (C) twice

    (D) blood

199. AQU : WATER :: IGNIS : _____

    (A) earth

    (B) light

    (C) fire

    (D) knowledge

200. CONTRACTION : _____ :: -STALSIS : -STASIS

    (A) stopping

    (B) inversion

    (C) pushing

    (D) dripping

CHAPTER 5

Classification Analogies

In this kind of analogy, one word in each pair is the category into which the other word falls. If A is to B as C is to D, and A is a category, then B is an example of something within that category, as in DOCTOR : SURGEON.

201. APPLIQUÉ : STITCHERY :: _____ : PRINTMAKING

- (A) intaglio
- (B) computer
- (C) embroidery
- (D) Gutenberg

202. COACH : CONVEYANCE :: ROACH : _____

- (A) vehicle
- (B) filth
- (C) insect
- (D) repulsion

203. ADA : ARF :: _____ : ONOMATOPOEIA

- (A) sound
- (B) girl
- (C) palindrome
- (D) lawyer

204. WEIMERANER : DOG :: _____ : HORSE

- (A) Percheron
- (B) Manx
- (C) Wyandotte
- (D) Pomeranian

205. STIMULANT : _____ :: DEPRESSANT : ALCOHOL

    (A) sedative

    (B) marijuana

    (C) morphine

    (D) caffeine

206. NOVEL : NOVELLA :: *LES MISERABLES* : _____

    (A) *Madame Bovary*

    (B) *Candide*

    (C) *The Count of Monte Cristo*

    (D) *The Red and the Black*

207. _____ : QUADRILATERAL :: SQUARE : RECTANGLE

    (A) trapezoid

    (B) equilateral

    (C) prism

    (D) heptagon

208. PUFFIN : PUFFBALL :: BIRD : _____

    (A) birdhouse

    (B) reptile

    (C) fern

    (D) fungus

209. CATHEDRAL : _____ :: MOSQUE : QOLSHARIF

    (A) Beit T'shuva

    (B) Notre Dame

    (C) Chichen Itza

    (D) San Luis Obispo

210. _____ : POTTERY :: FRESCO : PAINTING

    (A) amphora

    (B) tempera

    (C) banig

    (D) pipette

211. STUDEBAKER : AUTOMOBILE :: OLD TOWN : _____

- (A) motorcycle
- (B) canoe
- (C) yacht
- (D) truck

212. GLUCOSE : SUGAR :: ETHANOL : _____

- (A) oil
- (B) gas
- (C) salt
- (D) alcohol

213. GREAT LAKES : _____ :: HURON : CAYUGA

- (A) small lakes
- (B) Finger Lakes
- (C) Salt Lakes
- (D) rivers

214. DAKOTA : SIOUX :: HOPI : _____

- (A) Zuni
- (B) Seminole
- (C) Quinnipiac
- (D) Pueblo

215. _____ : TROMBONE :: WOODWIND : BRASS

- (A) cornet
- (B) tuba
- (C) saxophone
- (D) French horn

216. ADVERB : NOUN :: KINDLY : _____

- (A) kinder
- (B) kindle
- (C) kindness
- (D) kindhearted

217. BORON : ELEMENT :: BORAX : _____

    (A) atom

    (B) metal

    (C) compound

    (D) ion

218. _____ : CONFEDERATION :: SPARTA : HEGEMONY

    (A) United Arab Republic

    (B) Athens

    (C) Prussia

    (D) Carthage

219. CARTILAGINOUS : _____ :: BONY : EEL

    (A) trout

    (B) shark

    (C) coelacanth

    (D) sturgeon

220. ELIZABETH I : ELIZABETH II :: TUDOR : _____

    (A) Stuart

    (B) Wessex

    (C) Lancaster

    (D) Windsor

221. _____ : OLD TESTAMENT :: REVELATION : NEW TESTAMENT

    (A) Jude

    (B) Hebrews

    (C) Acts

    (D) Malachi

222. ORGANIC : _____ :: INORGANIC : AMMONIA
  - (A) salt
  - (B) sugar
  - (C) diamond
  - (D) water

223. "IF I HAD A HAMMER" : "UN BEL DI, VEDREMO" :: FOLK SONG :
_____
  - (A) lieder
  - (B) aria
  - (C) ballad
  - (D) hymn

224. NATIONAL PARK : NATIONAL FOREST :: ACADIA :
_____
  - (A) Olympia
  - (B) Badlands
  - (C) Denali
  - (D) Glacier

225. GULF : _____ :: AQABA : BENGAL
  - (A) sea
  - (B) strait
  - (C) bay
  - (D) canal

226. _____ : TITANS :: ZEUS : OLYMPIANS
  - (A) Jupiter
  - (B) Hera
  - (C) Kronos
  - (D) Neptune

227. _____ : GERMANY :: ALLIES : GREAT BRITAIN

    (A) Vichy

    (B) collaborators

    (C) Axis

    (D) Nazis

228. "30 ROCK" : SITCOM :: "GENERAL HOSPITAL" : _____

    (A) reality show

    (B) thriller

    (C) animation

    (D) soap opera

229. NIGER : _____ :: RIVER : CANAL

    (A) Rubicon

    (B) Rhine

    (C) Platte

    (D) Suez

230. _____ : SOPRANO :: PAVAROTTI : TENOR

    (A) Scotto

    (B) Carreras

    (C) Domingo

    (D) Anderson

231. _____ : OVINE :: TOM : FELINE

    (A) cow

    (B) ram

    (C) billy

    (D) bull

232. GYMNOSPERM : ANGIOSPERM :: _____ : OAK

    (A) pine

    (B) algae

    (C) maple

    (D) corn

233. _____ : WINTER OLYMPICS :: GYMNASTICS : SUMMER OLYMPICS

  (A) diving

  (B) biathlon

  (C) wrestling

  (D) rugby

234. WHALE : SHARK :: BALEEN : _____

  (A) dogfish

  (B) beluga

  (C) lamprey

  (D) minke

235. CARROTS : ROOTS :: _____ : BULBS

  (A) brussels sprouts

  (B) onions

  (C) parsnips

  (D) ginger

236. SHOAT : PIG :: CYGNET : _____

  (A) swan

  (B) stork

  (C) swallow

  (D) sandpiper

237. EPISTOLARY : PICARESQUE :: _____ : _The History of Tom Jones, a Foundling_

  (A) _Emma_

  (B) _Jane Eyre_

  (C) _Daisy Miller_

  (D) _Pamela_

238. ECRU : BEIGE :: CHARTREUSE : _____

    (A) red

    (B) yellow

    (C) orange

    (D) green

239. DAIRY : GRAIN :: _____ : BARLEY

    (A) ricotta

    (B) cashew

    (C) tofu

    (D) muesli

240. INDO-EUROPEAN : GERMANIC :: AFRO-ASIATIC : _____

    (A) Celtic

    (B) Aleut

    (C) Semitic

    (D) Khmer

241. COURBET : REALISM :: _____ : IMPRESSIONISM

    (A) Munch

    (B) Renoir

    (C) Bacon

    (D) Millet

242. _____ : FROG :: REPTILE : AMPHIBIAN

    (A) turtle

    (B) newt

    (C) spring peeper

    (D) eft

243. _____ : WOOL :: SHANTUNG : SILK

    (A) weave

    (B) worsted

    (C) viscose

    (D) sheep

244. POLYNESIAN : SAMOAN :: CHINESE : _____

   (A) Thai

   (B) Tahitian

   (C) Cantonese

   (D) Confucianism

245. EXECUTIVE : LEGISLATIVE :: HOMELAND SECURITY :

_____

   (A) Sentencing Commission

   (B) National Security Council

   (C) Library of Congress

   (D) Department of Commerce

246. JACK : DONKEY :: BULL : _____

   (A) badger

   (B) hog

   (C) antelope

   (D) alligator

247. TERRITORY : PROVINCE :: _____ : MANITOBA

   (A) Yukon

   (B) Winnipeg

   (C) Nova Scotia

   (D) Quebec

248. VERTEBRATE : INVERTEBRATE :: SNAKE : _____

   (A) bat

   (B) shrew

   (C) scorpion

   (D) eft

249. THALIA : GRACES :: CLOTHO : _____

   (A) Fates
   (B) Muses
   (C) Horae
   (D) Danaids

250. _____ : BEAN :: MONOCOT : DICOT

   (A) spinach
   (B) beet
   (C) corn
   (D) potato

CHAPTER 6

Part/Whole Analogies

In most part/whole analogies, one word in each pair is part of the other. In occasional part/whole analogies, each pair consists of parts of a whole, but the two wholes are unrelated. For example, in WATTLE : BEAK :: SCALE : FIN, both elements of the first pair are parts of a turkey and both elements of the second pair are parts of a fish.

251. COUNTY : NEW YORK :: PARISH : _____
- (A) priest
- (B) church
- (C) Louisiana
- (D) Colombia

252. MAJORCA : SPAIN :: CORSICA : _____
- (A) Sicily
- (B) France
- (C) Italy
- (D) Portugal

253. IRS : OSHA :: TREASURY : _____
- (A) State
- (B) FDA
- (C) Labor
- (D) HUD

254. WINGERS : RUGBY :: _____ : HOCKEY
- (A) forwards
- (B) midfielders
- (C) wings
- (D) receivers

255. _____ : DEER :: PREHENSILE TAIL : MONKEY

(A) scut

(B) retrices

(C) empennage

(D) plait

256. FORK : _____ :: SPOON : BOWL

(A) blade

(B) tine

(C) pitchfork

(D) plate

257. OPERA : ACT :: SYMPHONY : _____

(A) instrument

(B) bar

(C) prelude

(D) movement

258. FIBULA : TIBIA :: RADIUS : _____

(A) scapula

(B) phalange

(C) clavicle

(D) ulna

259. PERCUSSION : _____ :: WIND : HORN

(A) band

(B) beat

(C) cymbal

(D) marching

260. FOOT : PINT :: _____ : CUP

(A) leg

(B) quart

(C) meter

(D) inch

261. WHEELHOUSE : TUGBOAT :: _____ : JET

    (A) airport

    (B) cockpit

    (C) pilot

    (D) propeller

262. _____ : GOAT :: HARPY : BIRD

    (A) faun

    (B) nanny

    (C) sileni

    (D) donkey

263. _____ : PURPLE :: YELLOW : ORANGE

    (A) green

    (B) blue

    (C) lavender

    (D) royal

264. JAPAN : PREFECTURES :: SWITZERLAND : _____

    (A) departments

    (B) provinces

    (C) territories

    (D) cantons

265. BICYCLE : FRAME :: CANOE : _____

    (A) hull

    (B) oar

    (C) canvas

    (D) scaffold

266. _____ : TOE :: PALM : THUMB

    (A) limb

    (B) foot

    (C) ankle

    (D) arch

267. TESSERAE : _____ :: PIXELS : DIGITAL PHOTO

    (A) collage

    (B) tile

    (C) mosaic

    (D) transparency

268. SUMATRA : HONSHU :: INDONESIA : _____

    (A) Japan

    (B) Hawaii

    (C) New Zealand

    (D) Tonga

269. FRANCE : EU :: RUSSIA : _____

    (A) NATO

    (B) UAR

    (C) NAFTA

    (D) UN

270. CUBE : _____ :: PYRAMID : TRIANGLE

    (A) prism

    (B) square

    (C) cone

    (D) rectangle

271. AVARICE : ENVY :: EUCHARIST : _____

    (A) penance

    (B) lust

    (C) mystery

    (D) celebration

272. CHAMBER : REVOLVER :: BORE : _____

    (A) cannon

    (B) tunnel

    (C) trencher

    (D) gut

273. STOMACH : _____ :: WINE BOTTLE : CORK

- (A) intestine
- (B) food
- (C) sphincter
- (D) absorption

274. COLLEGE : _____ :: UNIVERSITY : PARLIAMENT

- (A) legislature
- (B) chamber
- (C) oligarchy
- (D) senate

275. UNION : CONFEDERACY :: _____ : ALABAMA

- (A) Tennessee
- (B) Arkansas
- (C) Ohio
- (D) Texas

276. CAP : _____ :: SPEAR : ASPARAGUS

- (A) root
- (B) eggplant
- (C) mushroom
- (D) pepper

277. ISLAND : MOUNTAIN :: ATOLL : _____

- (A) hill
- (B) Alp
- (C) vale
- (D) range

278. MANTEL : _____ :: FIREPLACE : DOORWAY

- (A) cannel
- (B) pommel
- (C) runnel
- (D) lintel

279. CARROT : ROOT HAIR :: LIVERWORT : _____

  (A) bryophyte
  (B) moss
  (C) rhizoid
  (D) seed

280. BOOK : HINGE :: SPINE : _____

  (A) gate
  (B) skull
  (C) nut
  (D) pin

281. BRASS : COPPER :: _____ : IRON

  (A) aluminum
  (B) steel
  (C) nickel
  (D) tungsten

282. FENCING : PENTATHLON :: _____ : DECATHLON

  (A) pole vaulting
  (B) swimming
  (C) archery
  (D) equestrian show jumping

283. MULLIGATAWNY : BORSCHT :: _____ : BEETROOT

  (A) kale
  (B) ramen
  (C) okra
  (D) curry

284. EASEL : CROSSBAR :: SAIL : _____

  (A) hatch
  (B) boom
  (C) jib
  (D) rope

285. _____ : CONSTANTINOPLE :: HOLY ROMAN EMPIRE : OTTOMAN EMPIRE

(A) Prague
(B) Rome
(C) Athens
(D) Paris

286. VITREOUS HUMOR : EYE :: _____ : SPINAL CORD

(A) gray matter
(B) lens
(C) vertebra
(D) column

287. SPIRACLES : _____ :: GILLS : FISH

(A) grasshopper
(B) palmetto
(C) oyster
(D) moss

288. _____ : MENNONITES :: MUSLIMS : SUNNI

(A) Catholics
(B) Presbyterians
(C) Anabaptists
(D) Lutherans

289. TAIL : _____ :: BAR : A

(A) Q
(B) R
(C) S
(D) T

290. PARIETAL LOBE : CAUDATE LOBE :: _____ : LIVER

(A) spinal cord
(B) cerebrum
(C) vision
(D) gall bladder

291. CORPS : DIVISION :: _____ : BATTALION

    (A) troops

    (B) regiment

    (C) platoon

    (D) navy

292. BEAUMONT : _____ :: GILBERT : SULLIVAN

    (A) Mulligan

    (B) Beauchamp

    (C) Fletcher

    (D) Hart

293. SENTENCE : PARAGRAPH :: _____ : STANZA

    (A) poem

    (B) paragraph

    (C) verse

    (D) line

294. MURDER : CROW :: SETT : _____

    (A) trap

    (B) badger

    (C) fox

    (D) otter

295. WALLPAPER : COMPUTER SCREEN :: _____ : COAT OF ARMS

    (A) field

    (B) shield

    (C) armor

    (D) carpet

296. _____ : SYMPHONY :: QUATRAIN : BALLAD

    (A) sonata

    (B) composer

    (C) verse

    (D) triad

297. CEREAL : SERIAL :: _____ : EPISODE

    (A) breakfast

    (B) spoon

    (C) bran

    (D) box

298. PHALANX : _____ :: MANDIBLE : JAW

    (A) esophagus

    (B) sternum

    (C) shoulder

    (D) finger

299. BIT : BYTE :: _____ : GALLON

    (A) cup

    (B) pint

    (C) quart

    (D) liter

300. SALIVARY GLANDS : GASTRIC GLANDS :: MOUTH : _____

    (A) esophagus

    (B) stomach

    (C) small intestine

    (D) liver

CHAPTER 7

Conversion Analogies

Conversion analogies take many forms. Sometimes, one word in each pair is a name for another, as in the Greek and Roman names for the same gods. Occasionally, one word is a different grammatical form of another. Rarely, one word contains the same letters, rearranged, as the other word in the pair. Conversion analogies may also be mathematical. For example, one term in the pair may be a fraction of the other, creating a complete mathematical ratio, as in 2 : 4 :: 3 : 6.

301. 4 : 5 :: 64 : _____
  (A) 25
  (B) 50
  (C) 75
  (D) 125

302. _____ : NEPTUNE :: HERMES : POSEIDON
  (A) Mercury
  (B) Mars
  (C) Jove
  (D) Hephaestus

303. CU : _____ :: COPPER : IRON
  (A) Io
  (B) Rh
  (C) Fe
  (D) Ir

304. ABYSSINIA : _____ :: SOUTH-WEST AFRICA : NAMIBIA

    (A) Libya
    (B) Egypt
    (C) Ethiopia
    (D) Iran

305. _____ : EOS :: PLUTO : HADES

    (A) Aurora
    (B) Fortuna
    (C) Diana
    (D) Luna

306. CHE : ERNESTO GUEVARA :: WILD BILL : _____

    (A) William Frederick Cody
    (B) Henry McCarty
    (C) James Butler Hickok
    (D) William Jefferson Clinton

307. 2/5 : 3/7 :: _____ : 7/3

    (A) 4/5
    (B) 7/5
    (C) 5/2
    (D) 1/5

308. _____ : AMP :: DIET : TIDE

    (A) volt
    (B) electricity
    (C) map
    (D) dampness

309. AIX LA CHAPPELLE : AACHEN :: BOMBAY : _____

    (A) Kolkata
    (B) Jaipur
    (C) Pune
    (D) Mumbai

310. 10 : 100 :: _____ : 400

    (A) 4

    (B) 5

    (C) 8

    (D) 40

311. TOKYO : EDO :: HO CHI MINH CITY : _____

    (A) Saigon

    (B) Hanoi

    (C) Da Nang

    (D) Hué

312. _____ : DECAY :: ADOPTED : DECOY

    (A) rotten

    (B) adapted

    (C) red herring

    (D) fostered

313. _____ : HARRISON :: IKE : EISENHOWER

    (A) Teddy

    (B) Old Hickory

    (C) Tippecanoe

    (D) Henry

314. 0.75 : 0.80 :: 3/4 : _____

    (A) 3/5

    (B) 4/5

    (C) 5/6

    (D) 9/10

315. SIZE : NIGH :: _____ : NEIGH

    (A) night

    (B) sized

    (C) horse

    (D) seize

316. FORMOSA : TAIWAN :: CEYLON : _____

(A) Pakistan
(B) Sri Lanka
(C) Madagascar
(D) Tamil

317. _____ : THE DEERSLAYER :: CHRISTOPHER NEWMAN : THE AMERICAN

(A) Natty Bumppo
(B) James Fenimore Cooper
(C) Mohican
(D) Leatherstocking

318. BACTERIA : BACTERIUM :: DATA : _____

(A) date
(B) data
(C) datum
(D) item

319. LATER : DINER :: LATTER : _____

(A) lunch
(B) dinner
(C) donor
(D) litter

320. _____ : TEMPI :: CHORUS : CHORUSES

(A) temper
(B) tempo
(C) tempest
(D) temp

321. 100 : 212 :: 0 : _____

(A) 32
(B) 100
(C) 120
(D) 200

322. CRIMSON : _____ :: HARVARD : YALE

(A) Bulldogs

(B) Big Red

(C) Blue

(D) Tigers

323. FLUSH : FLASH :: MUSK : _____

(A) mosque

(B) scent

(C) tusk

(D) mask

324. NORTH TARRYTOWN, NY : SLEEPY HOLLOW, NY :: SING SING, NY : _____

(A) Ossining, NY

(B) Poughkeepsie, NY

(C) White Plains, NY

(D) New Paltz, NY

325. WHINE : _____ :: WRITE : RIGHT

(A) left

(B) howl

(C) correct

(D) wine

326. BUCKEYE : HAWKEYE :: OHIO : _____

(A) Maine

(B) Iowa

(C) Kentucky

(D) Colorado

327. © : ™ :: _____ : TRADEMARK

(A) circa

(B) company

(C) copyright

(D) center

328. FLOW : LOW :: _____ : LAW

    (A) laws

    (B) flux

    (C) flaw

    (D) low

329. CONSTANTINOPLE : _____ :: PEKING : BEIJING

    (A) Ankara

    (B) Tehran

    (C) Istanbul

    (D) Baghdad

330. 25 : 75 :: _____ : 90

    (A) 30

    (B) 65

    (C) 80

    (D) 85

331. _____ : JUPITER :: CRONUS : SATURN

    (A) Zeus

    (B) Atlas

    (C) Minerva

    (D) Prometheus

332. _____ : BRITISH HONDURAS :: GUYANA : BRITISH GUIANA

    (A) Honduras

    (B) Belize

    (C) Brunei

    (D) Botswana

333. Δ : DELTA :: Γ : _____

    (A) tau

    (B) gamma

    (C) phi

    (D) lambda

334. VILLE-MARIE : _____ :: YORK : TORONTO

 (A) Ottawa
 (B) Montreal
 (C) Regina
 (D) Quebec City

335. 22 : 33 :: 44 : _____

 (A) 56
 (B) 60
 (C) 66
 (D) 88

336. _____ : THE GREAT :: IVAN IV : THE TERRIBLE

 (A) Frederick II
 (B) Henry II
 (C) Philip II
 (D) George II

337. FURY : HOLY :: _____ : HOLLY

 (A) ire
 (B) Noël
 (C) hallowed
 (D) furry

338. BEETHOVEN'S THIRD : BEETHOVEN'S SIXTH :: EROICA :

_____

 (A) Pastoral
 (B) Choral
 (C) Pathétique
 (D) Moonlight

339. OLD KINDERHOOK : MARTIN VAN BUREN :: OLD ROUGH
AND READY : _____

 (A) Zachary Taylor
 (B) Abraham Lincoln
 (C) Ulysses S. Grant
 (D) Chester A. Arthur

340. _____ : ZIMBABWE :: FRENCH SUDAN : MALI

   (A) Rhodesia
   (B) Zambia
   (C) Gold Coast
   (D) Zaire

341. JUNO : HERA :: BACCHUS : _____

   (A) Lucifer
   (B) Heracles
   (C) Dionysus
   (D) Satyr

342. 1/64 : 1/8 :: 0.016 : _____

   (A) 0.25
   (B) 0.025
   (C) 0.125
   (D) 0.32

343. _____ : BANGLADESH :: BURMA : MYANMAR

   (A) Siam
   (B) Kampuchea
   (C) Côte d'Ivoire
   (D) East Pakistan

344. $\alpha : \phi$ :: ALPHA : _____

   (A) phi
   (B) theta
   (C) psi
   (D) omega

345. UCLA : _____ :: USC : TROJANS

   (A) Knights
   (B) Tritons
   (C) Bruins
   (D) Flames

346. LOUSE : BISON :: LICE : _____

(A) boson
(B) bisons
(C) buffalo
(D) bison

347. JUDY GARLAND : _____ :: MARILYN MONROE : NORMA JEAN BAKER

(A) Frances Gumm
(B) Judith Tuvim
(C) Shirley Beaty
(D) Ruby Stevens

348. VENUS : MARS :: _____ : ARES

(A) Artemis
(B) Athena
(C) Aphrodite
(D) Minerva

349. RICHARD I : THE LIONHEARTED :: ETHELRED II :

_____

(A) the Peaceable
(B) the Martyr
(C) the Unready
(D) the Confessor

350. * : . . . :: ASTERISK : _____

(A) em space
(B) ellipses
(C) dash
(D) omission

CHAPTER 8

Characteristic Analogies

In this type of analogy, one word in each pair may be a description of the other, the location of the other, a material from which the other is made, a feature of the other, or even a feature that the other lacks.

351. NORTH AMERICA : SOUTH AMERICA :: _____ : PAMPAS

(A) Rockies

(B) states

(C) prairies

(D) borders

352. CLIO : URANIA :: _____ : ASTRONOMY

(A) advertising

(B) history

(C) literature

(D) astrology

353. GOSPELS : BIOGRAPHIES :: REVELATION : _____

(A) autobiography

(B) covenant

(C) fantasy

(D) prophecy

354. UNIVERSITY OF VIRGINIA : _____ :: UNIVERSITY OF PENNSYLVANIA : PHILADELPHIA

(A) Manassas

(B) Fredericksburg

(C) Charlottesville

(D) Norfolk

355. VOLUNTARY : INVOLUNTARY :: SKELETAL : _____

   (A) contracting

   (B) cardiac

   (C) protein

   (D) soft tissue

356. BÉCHAMEL : _____ :: MORNAY : CHEESE

   (A) roux

   (B) fish

   (C) tomato

   (D) onion

357. SPANISH : CUBA :: FRENCH : _____

   (A) Grenada

   (B) Haiti

   (C) Brazil

   (D) St. Thomas

358. PERIDOT : _____ :: GARNET : RED

   (A) green

   (B) orange

   (C) blue

   (D) silver

359. MONARCHY : PLUTOCRACY :: KING : _____

   (A) army

   (B) despot

   (C) wealthy

   (D) emperor

360. _____ : LONDON :: PRADO : MADRID

   (A) Hermitage

   (B) Kirchner

   (C) Holburne

   (D) Tate

361. SOLOMON : WISDOM :: _____ : STRENGTH

   (A) Abraham
   (B) Samson
   (C) Aaron
   (D) Joshua

362. DECLARATION OF INDEPENDENCE : 1776 :: _____ : 1848

   (A) Emancipation Proclamation
   (B) Homestead Act
   (C) Seneca Falls Declaration
   (D) Declaration of the Rights of Man

363. FARRAGUT : NAVY :: _____ : ARMY

   (A) Decatur
   (B) Sherman
   (C) Perry
   (D) Rickover

364. EISENHOWER : TEXAN :: _____ : CALIFORNIAN

   (A) Johnson
   (B) Reagan
   (C) Bush
   (D) Nixon

365. EUKARYOTIC : PROKARYOTIC :: FISH : _____

   (A) moss
   (B) tree
   (C) bird
   (D) bacterium

366. _____ : PARIS :: MICHELANGELO'S *DAVID* : FLORENCE

(A) Leonardo's *Horse*

(B) *Eros*

(C) Winged Victory

(D) *Pieta*

367. CHLOROPHYLL : SPINACH :: CAROTENOID : _____

(A) fruit flies

(B) cabbage

(C) carrots

(D) soybeans

368. OCD : ANXIETY :: _____ : HALLUCINATIONS

(A) schizophrenia

(B) pyromania

(C) arachnophobia

(D) mood disorder

369. _____ : CIRRUS :: PUFFY : CUMULUS

(A) wispy

(B) vertical

(C) dark

(D) bulbous

370. GOITER : _____ :: SCURVY : VITAMIN C

(A) vitamin D

(B) beriberi

(C) iodine

(D) iron

371. VODKA : _____ :: RUM : MOLASSES

(A) grapes

(B) honey

(C) sugar beets

(D) potatoes

372. _____ : EVEN-TOED :: HORSE : ODD-TOED

    (A) giraffe

    (B) rhinoceros

    (C) burro

    (D) zebra

373. CONCHO : SILVER :: CORNET : _____

    (A) brass

    (B) gray

    (C) wood

    (D) iron

374. MAPLE LEAF : _____ :: DNA : HELICAL

    (A) elliptical

    (B) linear

    (C) palmate

    (D) deltoid

375. FORT MCHENRY : _____ :: FORT SUMTER : CIVIL WAR

    (A) French and Indian War

    (B) American Revolution

    (C) War of 1812

    (D) Spanish-American War

376. GLIDER : MOTOR :: INTEGRATED CIRCUIT : _____

    (A) transistor

    (B) wires

    (C) crystal

    (D) semiconductor

377. CHILE : PESO :: SAUDI ARABIA : _____

    (A) pound

    (B) dinar

    (C) riyal

    (D) dollar

378. METAL : _____ :: NONMETAL : BRITTLE

  (A) malleable
  (B) transparent
  (C) nonconductive
  (D) golden

379. SANDSTONE : BASALT :: TAN : _____

  (A) white
  (B) brown
  (C) streaked
  (D) black

380. _____ : HATCHING :: DOTS : LINES

  (A) intaglio
  (B) quilting
  (C) stippling
  (D) soufflage

381. KARATE : TAI CHI :: JAPAN : _____

  (A) China
  (B) Korea
  (C) Malaysia
  (D) Nepal

382. _____ : WIND :: STALEMATE : MOVEMENT

  (A) airstream
  (B) gale
  (C) doldrums
  (D) current

383. TIN MAN : _____ :: LION : COURAGE

  (A) intelligence
  (B) compassion
  (C) fear
  (D) generosity

384. FIXED HEEL : FREE HEEL :: ALPINE : _____

- (A) Nordic
- (B) downhill
- (C) slalom
- (D) racing

385. _____ : ONION DOME :: ST. PETER'S BASILICA : UMBRELLA DOME

- (A) Taj Mahal
- (B) Pantheon
- (C) US Capitol
- (D) Astrodome

386. ELLESMERE : ARCTIC OCEAN :: _____ : INDIAN OCEAN

- (A) Ibiza
- (B) Malta
- (C) Vanuatu
- (D) Sumatra

387. _____ : SPEED :: VENUS : BEAUTY

- (A) Ulysses
- (B) Vulcan
- (C) Mercury
- (D) Apollo

388. MAMBO : _____ :: TANGO : ARGENTINA

- (A) Cuba
- (B) Brazil
- (C) Haiti
- (D) Jamaica

389. PORCELAIN : KAOLIN :: TAPESTRY : _____

  (A) loom
  (B) France
  (C) wool
  (D) weft

390. COYOTE : _____ :: BULL : POWERFUL

  (A) helpful
  (B) tricky
  (C) weak
  (D) naive

391. NEOCLASSICAL : SYMMETRICAL :: ITALIANATE :

_____

  (A) vertical
  (B) unadorned
  (C) blocky
  (D) rounded

392. TISSUE : _____ :: TRANSLUCENT : OPAQUE

  (A) wood
  (B) glass
  (C) gauze
  (D) net

393. IMPETIGO : SKIN :: PHLEBITIS : _____

  (A) limb
  (B) skull
  (C) vein
  (D) sinus

394. BACH : _____ :: BAROQUE : CLASSICAL

  (A) Chopin
  (B) Schubert
  (C) Beethoven
  (D) Purcell

395. SNAKE : _____ :: SCALE : SCUTE

    (A) turtle

    (B) horse

    (C) rhinoceros

    (D) duck

396. SCOTTISH : RUSSIAN :: HIGHLANDS : _____

    (A) savannas

    (B) highvelds

    (C) rain forests

    (D) steppes

397. FINGERNAIL : _____ :: HOBNAIL : IRON

    (A) bone

    (B) phalanx

    (C) keratin

    (D) cartilage

398. MECCA : MUHAMMAD :: _____ : JESUS

    (A) Jerusalem

    (B) Bethlehem

    (C) Nazareth

    (D) Calvary

399. NORTHERN HEMISPHERE : SOUTHERN HEMISPHERE :: _____ : AUSTRALIA

    (A) Peru

    (B) India

    (C) Tanzania

    (D) Fiji

400. LION : MANE :: TURKEY : _____

    (A) carbuncle

    (B) spur

    (C) feather

    (D) beard

CHAPTER 9

Sequence Analogies

This kind of analogy involves a sequence that may be numerical, verbal, process-related, or familial (generational, for example).

401. ABRAHAM : _____ :: ZEUS : APOLLO
   (A) Ra
   (B) God
   (C) Moses
   (D) Isaac

402. CONTRALTO : MEZZO-SOPRANO :: _____ : BARITONE
   (A) tenor
   (B) alto
   (C) bass
   (D) countertenor

403. EST : PST :: _____ : 4:00
   (A) 7:00
   (B) 3:00
   (C) 1:00
   (D) 10:00

404. WILHELM : WILBUR :: _____ : ORVILLE
   (A) Henry
   (B) Frank
   (C) Richard
   (D) Jacob

405. FILLY : MARE :: _____ : OYSTER

    (A) pearl

    (B) nymph

    (C) spat

    (D) squab

406. REHEARSALS : PERFORMANCE :: PROTOTYPES : _____

    (A) mockup

    (B) pilot

    (C) challenge

    (D) product

407. NOVEMBER : OCTOBER :: WEDNESDAY : _____

    (A) Thursday

    (B) weekend

    (C) Tuesday

    (D) Sunday

408. ERIC THE RED : LEIF ERICSSON :: HENRY VIII : _____

    (A) Henry VII

    (B) Elizabeth I

    (C) Anne Boleyn

    (D) James I

409. FRAMEWORK : SKYSCRAPER :: CHARTER : _____

    (A) agenda

    (B) government

    (C) route

    (D) participant

410. 1 : 10 :: _____ : 100

    (A) 01

    (B) 110

    (C) 101

    (D) 11

411. BATTLE OF LEXINGTON AND CONCORD : _____ ::
BATTLE OF FORT SUMTER : BATTLE OF COLUMBUS

(A) Battle of Gettysburg
(B) Battle of Stoney Creek
(C) Battle of Yorktown
(D) Battle of Manila Bay

412. EGG : LARVA :: _____ : IMAGO

(A) pupa
(B) embryo
(C) caterpillar
(D) blastocyst

413. SEEK : FIND :: ASK : _____

(A) collect
(B) query
(C) appear
(D) receive

414. ORANGE : YELLOW :: INDIGO : _____

(A) blue
(B) violet
(C) green
(D) black

415. _____ : MAIN SEQUENCE :: RED GIANT :
WHITE DWARF

(A) protostar
(B) black hole
(C) supernova
(D) red supergiant

416. 3 : 5 :: _____ : 11

    (A) 4
    (B) 7
    (C) 8
    (D) 10

417. LEAR : CORDELIA :: PROSPERO : _____

    (A) Regan
    (B) Olivia
    (C) Miranda
    (D) Gertrude

418. DELTA : EPSILON :: SIGMA : _____

    (A) rho
    (B) tau
    (C) gamma
    (D) kappa

419. _____ : HYPOTHESIS :: TEST : ANALYSIS

    (A) communication
    (B) conclusion
    (C) question
    (D) variable

420. _____ : HAWAII :: A : Z

    (A) Alaska
    (B) Maine
    (C) Florida
    (D) Delaware

421. NILE : _____ :: MOUNT EVEREST : K2

    (A) Mississippi
    (B) Amazon
    (C) Yangtze
    (D) Niger

422. ANNE BOLEYN : ELIZABETH I :: _____ : MARY SHELLEY

(A) Mary Wollstonecraft
(B) Emmeline Pankhurst
(C) Marie Antoinette
(D) Marie Curie

423. _____ : WAS :: HAVE : HAD

(A) am
(B) were
(C) been
(D) have been

424. MR. BENNETT : ELIZABETH :: MR. CRATCHIT : _____

(A) Bob
(B) Ebenezer
(C) Charles
(D) Tim

425. _____ : POSTWAR :: INJURY : POSTTRAUMATIC

(A) hostilities
(B) damage
(C) wound
(D) ambush

426. _____ : THYMINE :: GUANINE : CYTOSINE

(A) adipose
(B) adenine
(C) thyroxin
(D) edentate

427. XX : L :: CC : _____

(A) D
(B) M
(C) LL
(D) CD

428. PAST : FUTURE :: YESTERDAY : _____

    (A) now

    (B) weekend

    (C) forever

    (D) tomorrow

429. PALEOZOIC : MESOZOIC :: _____ : TRIASSIC

    (A) Permian

    (B) Jurassic

    (C) Cretaceous

    (D) Quaternary

430. Q : _____ :: Y : X

    (A) P

    (B) T

    (C) A

    (D) R

431. _____ : HAGAR :: HAMLET : GERTRUDE

    (A) Abram

    (B) Joshua

    (C) David

    (D) Ishmael

432. KENNEDY : JOHNSON :: _____ : FORD

    (A) Carter

    (B) Nixon

    (C) Reagan

    (D) Dole

433. BOAR : BEAR :: _____ : CUB

    (A) pullet

    (B) sow

    (C) calf

    (D) shoat

434. GIGA- : _____ :: MILLI- : MICRO-

    (A) MEGA-
    (B) CENTI-
    (C) TERA-
    (D) KILO-

435. TRIANGLE : RECTANGLE :: PENTAGON : _____

    (A) hexagon
    (B) circle
    (C) octagon
    (D) heptagon

436. _____ : LENT :: CHRISTMAS : EASTER

    (A) New Year
    (B) Boxing Day
    (C) Advent
    (D) gifted

437. _____ : D :: G : A

    (A) C
    (B) E
    (C) F
    (D) B

438. 1 : HYDROGEN :: 2 : _____

    (A) water
    (B) helium
    (C) oxygen
    (D) nitrogen

439. CUP : _____ :: QUART : HALF GALLON

    (A) ounce
    (B) spoon
    (C) pint
    (D) liter

440. ABACUS : CALCULATOR :: _____ : E-BOOK

  (A) counting
  (B) cell phone
  (C) book
  (D) electronics

441. _____ : 1/8 :: 1/16 : 1/32

  (A) 1/16
  (B) 1/4
  (C) 1/7
  (D) 1/18

442. ALPHA : OMEGA :: GENESIS : _____

  (A) Exodus
  (B) Psalms
  (C) Revelation
  (D) Romans

443. KINGDOM : _____ :: GENUS : SPECIES

  (A) class
  (B) order
  (C) phylum
  (D) family

444. _____ : ANDANTE :: SLOW : MODERATE

  (A) adagio
  (B) piano
  (C) animato
  (D) allegro

445. VICTORIA : EDWARD VII :: _____ : ELIZABETH II

  (A) GEORGE V
  (B) EDWARD VII
  (C) GEORGE VI
  (D) CHARLES

446. _____ : CHURCHILL :: THATCHER : MAJOR

(A) Chamberlain

(B) Blair

(C) Wilson

(D) Heath

447. AIM : FIRE :: _____ : DRINK

(A) bottle

(B) pour

(C) wine

(D) swallow

448. PARR : _____ :: TADPOLE : FROG

(A) newt

(B) rabbit

(C) salmon

(D) spider

449. _____ : FOXTROT :: NINETEENTH : TWENTIETH

(A) gavotte

(B) minuet

(C) polka

(D) two-step

450. ROMULUS : REMUS :: _____ : PARIS

(A) Achilles

(B) Seine

(C) Rome

(D) Hector

CHAPTER 10

Object/Action Analogies

In an object/action analogy, one word in each pair is an object or agent that causes or uses another. Often the relationship involves invention and creation, function, or cause and effect.

451. DEFOLIATE : DEFOREST :: _____ : TREES

(A) pages
(B) skin
(C) leaves
(D) woods

452. _____ : CHARLIE PARKER :: TRUMPET : SAXOPHONE

(A) Eartha Kitt
(B) Dizzy Gillespie
(C) New Orleans
(D) John Coltrane

453. LOUISIANA PURCHASE : GADSDEN PURCHASE :: _____ : MEXICO

(A) France
(B) Jefferson
(C) Louisiana
(D) England

454. LIVER : BILE :: KIDNEY : _____

(A) excrete
(B) stone
(C) ureter
(D) urine

455. REGISTRAR : PROVOST :: _____ : CURRICULUM

    (A) records

    (B) admissions

    (C) athletics

    (D) careers

456. PLAINTIFF : SUIT :: COURT : _____

    (A) lawyer

    (B) remedy

    (C) claim

    (D) fact

457. BOOKER PRIZE : _____ :: TONY : DRAMA

    (A) novel

    (B) TV show

    (C) poem

    (D) comedy

458. HYPOTHALAMUS : EMOTIONS :: _____ : BALANCE

    (A) cerebellum

    (B) cerebrum

    (C) pancreas

    (D) medulla

459. _____ : SPIRIT :: EXCISE : TUMOR

    (A) exist

    (B) lift

    (C) exorcise

    (D) hail

460. SPRINTER : HURDLE :: _____ : BAR

    (A) long jumper

    (B) race walker

    (C) miler

    (D) pole vaulter

461. RONALD REAGAN : _____ :: JOHN ADAMS : JOHN MARSHALL

(A) Alexander Haig
(B) George H. W. Bush
(C) Jimmy Carter
(D) William Rehnquist

462. 13 : 18 :: SLAVERY : _____

(A) enfranchisement
(B) weaponry
(C) alcohol
(D) states' rights

463. PHILIPPINE REVOLUTION : _____ :: AMERICAN REVOLUTION : ENGLAND

(A) Philippines
(B) Spain
(C) Manila
(D) China

464. EULOGY : PRAISE :: ELEGY : _____

(A) commend
(B) gratify
(C) censure
(D) lament

465. PERIODONTIST : _____ :: OPHTHALMOLOGIST : EYES

(A) feet
(B) ears
(C) gums
(D) lungs

466. UNITARIANISM : _____ :: ANGLICANISM : PAPACY

    (A) peace

    (B) Trinity

    (C) deity

    (D) community

467. ETHNOLOGIST : ETYMOLOGIST :: _____ : LANGUAGE

    (A) culture

    (B) speech

    (C) structure

    (D) government

468. _____ : STRAVINSKY :: CHOREOGRAPHY : COMPOSITION

    (A) Britten

    (B) Balanchine

    (C) Bernstein

    (D) Baryshnikov

469. BADEN-POWELL : _____ :: BOY SCOUTS : GIRL SCOUTS

    (A) Alcott

    (B) Stanton

    (C) Low

    (D) Mott

470. FARRIER : FURRIER :: _____ : HIDE

    (A) shoe

    (B) iron

    (C) beat

    (D) horse

471. ZENO : _____ :: ANTISTHENES : CYNICISM

    (A) Stoicism

    (B) Rationalism

    (C) Fauvism

    (D) Eclecticism

472. FLEUR-DE-LIS : _____ :: FRANCE : ENGLAND

    (A) lilac

    (B) daffodil

    (C) lion

    (D) dragon

473. FLEMING : JENNER :: PENICILLIN : _____

    (A) rabies vaccine

    (B) aspirin

    (C) tranquilizer

    (D) smallpox vaccine

474. ORTHOTIST : _____ :: RADIOLOGIST : X-RAY

    (A) tooth

    (B) sonogram

    (C) brace

    (D) membrane

475. *METAMORPHOSES* : *THE METAMORPHOSIS* :: _____ : KAFKA

    (A) Ovid

    (B) Virgil

    (C) Aeschylus

    (D) Sophocles

476. HERTZ : _____ :: OHM : RESISTANCE

    (A) tempo

    (B) volume

    (C) frequency

    (D) force

477. _____ : SORROW :: CURTSY : RESPECT

    (A) grief

    (B) tear

    (C) bereavement

    (D) bow

478. GREMLIN : MISCHIEF :: _____ : BEHEST

    (A) genie

    (B) leprechaun

    (C) jinx

    (D) goblin

479. EASTMAN : WESTINGHOUSE :: _____ : AIR BRAKE

    (A) brake light

    (B) cassette tape

    (C) film

    (D) radar

480. _____ : GOUGE :: MASON : TROWEL

    (A) plowman

    (B) woodcarver

    (C) chef

    (D) chimney sweep

481. RUBELLA : RASH :: _____ : LOCKJAW

    (A) mumps

    (B) tetanus

    (C) German measles

    (D) influenza

482. JOHN BOYD DUNLOP : _____ :: LINUS YALE :
CYLINDER LOCK

(A) mountain bike
(B) pneumatic tire
(C) catalytic converter
(D) motorcycle

483. THUMB : GRASPING :: _____ : SHOCK ABSORPTION

(A) fibula
(B) wrist
(C) arch
(D) ligament

484. _____ : JANE EYRE :: HAWTHORNE : BRONTË

(A) Emma Bovary
(B) Becky Sharp
(C) Moll Flanders
(D) Hester Prynne

485. HEART : CIRCULATE :: _____ : DEFEND

(A) lung
(B) pancreas
(C) lymph
(D) spine

486. CRINGE : FEAR :: SNEER : _____

(A) courage
(B) indifference
(C) contempt
(D) indignation

487. BURR : _____ :: SHEARS : PRUNING

(A) sticking
(B) sprinkling
(C) digging
(D) filing

488. _____ : CELLO :: ITZHAK PERLMAN : VIOLIN

    (A) Isaac Stern

    (B) Yehudi Menuhin

    (C) Yo Yo Ma

    (D) Pinchas Zukerman

489. HUDSON : NORTHEAST :: _____ : SOUTHWEST

    (A) Aviles

    (B) De Soto

    (C) Coronado

    (D) Vespucci

490. THEORY : _____ :: POEM : RECITE

    (A) collect

    (B) defer

    (C) peruse

    (D) expound

491. CONFESSOR : ASSESSOR :: _____ : EVALUATION

    (A) guilt

    (B) verdict

    (C) absolution

    (D) inscription

492. LADY CHATTERLEY : LADY WINDERMERE :: LAWRENCE : _____

    (A) Sheridan

    (B) Wilde

    (C) Thackery

    (D) Trollope

493. DAVID LIVINGSTONE : NILE RIVER :: MUNGO PARK :
_____

(A) Amazon River
(B) Mississippi River
(C) Niger River
(D) Ganges River

494. _____ : NEW ECONOMICS :: MAILER : NEW
JOURNALISM

(A) Marx
(B) Friedman
(C) Malthus
(D) Keynes

495. JUDGE : LAW :: ACTUARY : _____

(A) probability
(B) premium
(C) accident
(D) mathematics

496. _____ : BUSHEL :: DEPTH : VOLUME

(A) peck
(B) fathom
(C) cube
(D) width

497. MORSE : _____ :: LAND : PHOTOGRAPHY

(A) communication
(B) education
(C) oratory
(D) oceanography

498. NILE : MEDITERRANEAN :: MEKONG : _____

    (A) South China Sea

    (B) Indian Ocean

    (C) Coral Sea

    (D) Arabian Sea

499. _____ : AMMUNITION :: PICA : TYPE

    (A) shell

    (B) cannon

    (C) caliber

    (D) agate

500. SCALE : JUDGMENT :: _____ : LAST JUDGMENT

    (A) Kabbalah

    (B) pentacle

    (C) seven seals

    (D) Lion of Judah

ANSWERS

Chapter 1: Synonym Analogies

1. (B) If something is *damaged*, you might also say it is *spoiled*. If something is *fixed*, you might also say it is *refurbished*.

2. (D) A synonym for *candor* is *frankness*, and a synonym for *dander* is *temper*.

3. (C) Someone who is *humble* is *modest*. Someone who is a *humbug* is an *imposter*, or a fake. This analogy is in the form A is to C as B is to D.

4. (D) An obstacle may have *frustrated* or *thwarted* you. Something that is *tainted* is spoiled or *fouled*.

5. (A) To *uplift* is to *boost*, and to *thrash* is to *pummel*. This is another A is to C as B is to D analogy.

6. (A) A *miasma* is a *haze* or fog. A *cloudburst* is a heavy rain, or *downpour*.

7. (C) To *rotate* is to *revolve*, or turn around. To *dive* is to *plummet*, or drop downward.

8. (C) In poetry or prose, a *caesura* is a break or *pause* in a line. An *anaphora* is the *repetition* of a word or a phrase.

9. (C) Here the A and C elements are synonyms—a *fixative* is something that sticks things together, as is an *adhesive*. The B element that is synonymous with *lacquer* is *varnish*.

10. (A) A *drone* is like a *chant*—both are monotonous tones. A *guffaw* is like a *chortle*—both are delighted laughs.

11. (D) Elements A and B are synonyms—*fabricated* can mean the same thing as *constructed*. That means that element D must mean *doused*, and *immersed* comes closest.

12. (D) *Prior* means about the same thing as *heretofore*. *Nevertheless* means about the same thing as *yet*.

13. (B) If you *exonerate* someone, you *absolve* him or her of responsibility for a crime. If you *exorcise* evil spirits, you *expel* them from someone's soul.

14. (D) To *pollute* is to *adulterate*, or contaminate. To *elucidate* is to *clarify*, or explain.

15. (B) Here, elements B and D have similar meanings, so your choice must be a synonym for *radiance*. The best choice is *luminosity*.

16. (B) *Heresy* is similar to *sacrilege*; both are acts that go against religious orthodoxy. If you show *reverence* toward someone or something, that is the same as showing *veneration*.

17. (D) Certain French phrases have made their way into English usage. Examples include *faux pas,* which refers to a social *gaffe,* or error, and *idée fixe,* which is an *obsession.*

18. (A) *Despite* and *notwithstanding* are synonyms, as are *routinely* and *customarily.*

19. (A) To *pledge* is to *vouchsafe,* or promise. To *decry* is to *condemn,* or criticize.

20. (A) If you are *debonair,* or refined, you might also be called *suave.* If you are *valiant,* or intrepid, you might also be called *brave.*

21. (C) The Roman numeral for 4 is IV. The Roman numeral for 14 is XIV.

22. (C) A *polemic* is an impassioned argument, or a *diatribe.* Because elements A and C are synonyms, B and D must be synonyms, too. The best synonym for *postulate* in its noun form is *assertion*—a postulate is a sort of claim or hypothesis.

23. (B) An animal that is *ravenous* is *voracious,* or greedily hungry. A person who is *extravagant* is *profligate,* or excessively wasteful.

24. (D) A *tarn* is a *pond.* Since elements B and D are synonyms, elements A and C must be as well. Of the choices given, the best synonym for *bond* is *rapport.*

25. (D) A *gamut* is a *range,* as of colors or emotions. A *gamin* is a male *urchin,* or waif.

26. (C) Something that is *ubiquitous* is *omnipresent,* or available everywhere. Someone who is *almighty* is *omnipotent,* or all-powerful.

27. (D) *Reparation* is *compensation*, especially for an injury or wrong. A *separation* is a *partition*.

28. (C) To *rectify* is to *redress*, or correct a wrong. Since elements C and D are synonyms, you must find the best synonym for *recant*, which would be *disavow*.

29. (B) Something that is *onerous* is *burdensome*. Someone who is *perspicacious* is *insightful*.

30. (A) A *stigma* is a form of *dishonor*. An *enigma* is a form of *puzzle*.

31. (C) *Groundhog* and *woodchuck* are regional names for the same rodent. *Skunk* and *polecat* are regional names for the same mustelid.

32. (C) If you are *reticent*, you are *reserved*, or shy. A *reticule* is a small drawstring *purse*.

33. (C) If something is *visible*, it is *evident*, or apparent. If a situation is *risible*, it is *ludicrous*, or laughable.

34. (A) Although we use the French phrase *à la mode* to refer to ice cream with toppings, its real meaning is more general—it refers to the *trendy* fashion of the time. *Avant garde* is usually used to refer to *innovative* thinking or art.

35. (C) When you *exceed* expectations, you *outdo* what people expect. When you *supersede* your boss, you replace, or *supplant*, him or her.

36. (B) *Connection* and *correlation* are synonyms, as are *division* and *schism*.

37. (C) The *fourth estate* refers to the press. In the time of the French Revolution, the first estate was the clergy, the second estate the nobility, and the third estate the commoners. *Fifth column* was a term coined by a Nationalist general during the Spanish Civil War to refer to his clandestine supporters, or *subversives*, during an assault on Madrid by four of his army columns.

38. (D) *Impetus* and *momentum* both refer to the force that moves an object. *Inertia* and *inaction* both refer to the tendency of an object to remain at rest.

39. (A) To *gaze* is to *peer*, or look closely. To *yaw* is to *veer*, or turn sharply.

40. (D) To *facilitate* is to *enable*. Since elements B and D are synonyms, elements A and C must be synonyms. The best choice to match *beleaguer* is *harass*.

41. (B) Although you may be tempted to pair *seism* or *shock* with *temblor*, start by looking at the other elements in the analogy. Here, *temblor* already pairs with *earthquake*, so you must find the synonym for *inferno* instead. The best choice is *conflagration*.

42. (A) *Worrisome* and *disquieting* both mean "troubling." *Suspicious* and *dubious* both mean "mistrustful."

43. (B) The Latin phrase *ad libitum*, more commonly known as "ad lib," translates as "at pleasure." *Ad infinitum* translates as "to infinity."

44. (C) Something that is *fraudulent*, or fake, may be *counterfeit*. Something that is *flavorful*, or tasty, may be *savory*.

45. (C) *Arroyo* and *key* are both words from Spanish. The first is used to refer to a small gully or *gulch*. The second is another word for *island*.

46. (C) A substance that is *gelid* is *frozen*. A substance that is *pliable* is *elastic*.

47. (A) Since elements B and D are synonyms, look for the synonym for element C, *truncheon*. The best choice is *cudgel*—both refer to weapons used to beat.

48. (B) To be *blameworthy*, or guilty, is to be *reprehensible*. To be *plausible* is to be *logical*.

49. (B) A *violent* person or animal is *aggressive*. A *passive* person or animal is *submissive*.

50. (A) A sound that is deep and *resonant* is *sonorous*. A sound that is sharp and *strident* is *shrill*.

Chapter 2: Antonym Analogies

51. (A) The opposite of *dote*, or adore, is *neglect*. The opposite of *dotage*, or old age, is *youth*.

52. (B) *Adult* and *juvenile* are opposites. The same is true of *sham* (fake) and *bona fide* (real).

53. (B) To be *hale*, or healthy, is the opposite of being *ailing*. To be *neat* is the opposite of being *disorderly*.

54. (A) A *schism* is a split, or the opposite of a *union*. *Ennui* is boredom, or the opposite of *eagerness*.

55. (D) Someone who is *proficient* is clearly not *incompetent*, or lacking ability. Someone who is *effusive*, or loudly demonstrative, is clearly not *reticent*, or quietly discreet.

56. (D) The opposites given are *generous* and *stingy*, so you must find the antonym for *brash*. Someone who is *brash* is hasty and foolhardy, the opposite of *restrained*.

57. (B) To be *frantic* is the opposite of being *unruffled*. To be *bewildered* is the opposite of being *enlightened*.

58. (D) If you are *feverish*, you are hot rather than *chilly*. If you are *animated*, you are lively rather than *sluggish*.

59. (A) *Sour* is the opposite of *sugary*, and *soar* is the opposite of *plummet*, or fall.

60. (C) *Equanimity*, or calmness, is the opposite of *volatility*, or explosiveness. *Immobility*, or lack of motion, is the opposite of *motion*.

61. (B) If something is *uniform*, it is consistent rather than *inconsistent*. If something is *ambiguous*, it is not *obvious*.

62. (C) *Cacophony*, which means "terrible din," is the opposite of *euphony*, which means "pleasant sound." Similarly, *despair* is the opposite of *euphoria*.

63. (C) A *fool* is the opposite of a *sage*. A *fiend* (demon) is the opposite of a *seraph* (angel).

64. (D) In this case, the opposing words are A and C and B and D. *Chivalry* may refer to extreme politeness, or the opposite of *rudeness*. *Treachery* is disloyalty, the opposite of *loyalty*.

65. (A) Since *hauteur* and *hater* have nothing to do with each other, the analogy must be A to C and B to D. An *aficionado* is a fan, or the opposite of a *hater*. *Humility* is an unassuming quality, or the opposite of *hauteur*, which means "haughtiness" or "self-importance."

66. (A) If you *alter* something, you fail to *preserve* it. If you *falter* in a task, you fail to *persist* at it.

67. (A) Just as *gain* is the opposite of *loss*, in chemistry, *reduction* is the opposite of *oxidation*. In reduction, atoms gain electrons, and in oxidation, atoms lose electrons.

68. (D) Someone who is *agile* is not *maladroit*, or clumsy. Something that is *facile*, or superficial, is not *profound*.

69. (B) *Infirmity*, or ailment, is the opposite of *well-being*, or health. *Disparager*, or detractor, is the opposite of *well-wisher*.

70. (C) On a color wheel, *yellow* and *violet* are opposites, and *green* and *red* are opposites.

71. (D) On a compass, *east* lies opposite *west*, and *northeast* lies opposite *southwest*.

72. (C) The analogies here are A to C and B to D. *Retreat* is the opposite of *advance*, and *disguise* is the opposite of *unmask*.

73. (D) To be *pigheaded* is to be stubborn, or inflexible. To be *fishy* is to be suspect. The opposites for each are *flexible* and *above-board*, respectively.

74. (A) Something that *diminishes* grows smaller; something that *intensifies* grows larger. Someone who *discourages* fails to *motivate*.

75. (D) If you are *wrongheaded*, you are not very *astute*, or incisive. If you are *phlegmatic*, you are not very *energetic*.

76. (B) If something is *preponderant*, it is very common. If something is *predictable*, it is to be expected.

77. (B) The opposite of *fortunate* is *cataclysmic*, or disastrous. The opposite of *reputable* is *infamous*, or notorious.

78. (A) A *watertight* substance is not *permeable* to water. A *malleable* substance is flexible, not *firm*.

79. (A) *Mettle*, meaning "bravery," and *meddle*, meaning "interfere," have nothing to do with each other, so the analogies here must be A to C and B to D, making *cowardice* the best answer.

80. (D) If you are *green*, you are not *experienced*. If you are *jaded*, you are not *enthusiastic*.

81. (A) *Grandiloquent,* or long-winded, is the opposite of *straightforward. Graceful* is the opposite of *ungainly.*

82. (B) The *denouement* of a story is the ending, or the opposite of the *beginning.* The *finale* of a musical composition is the ending, or the opposite of the *prelude.*

83. (D) Someone who is *meticulous* is not *slipshod,* or careless. Someone who is *jejune,* or immature, is not *sophisticated.*

84. (C) A *mundane,* or ordinary, event is not *exotic.* A *servile,* or submissive, person is not *assertive.*

85. (B) The opposites here are A to C and B to D. *Oppressive,* meaning "domineering," may be the opposite of *lenient,* and *unlucky* may be the opposite of *auspicious.*

86. (D) To be *garrulous* is to talk a lot; to be *taciturn* is to talk very little. To be *articulate* is to express yourself clearly; to be *incoherent* is to be unable to express yourself.

87. (C) To be *fractious* is the opposite of being *even-tempered.* To be *unfair* is the opposite of being *evenhanded.*

88. (C) If you are *tenacious,* or stubborn, you are not *irresolute* (indecisive). If a theory is *tenable,* or plausible, it is not *unsound* (illogical).

89. (B) A *peon* is a member of a lower, or working class, and a *patrician* is a member of an upper, or noble class. The opposite of a *native* is an *alien,* or foreigner.

90. (A) The opposite of *suspect* is *trust,* and the opposite of *dissuade* is *encourage.*

91. (B) *Numbness* is the lack of *sensation,* and *concord* is the lack of *conflict.*

92. (B) Something that is *perpetual,* or ongoing, is not *provisional,* or short-term. Something that is *compulsory,* or required, is not *voluntary.*

93. (B) If you are *puerile,* or juvenile, you are not *mature.* If you are *pugnacious,* or antagonistic, you are not *peaceable.*

94. (C) If something is *poisonous,* it is anything but *innocuous,* or harmless. If someone is *hostile,* he or she is anything but *congenial,* or friendly.

95. (D) If something is not *unsullied*, it may be *tarnished*. If someone is not *accepted*, that person may be *banished*.

96. (D) *Maternal* relates to the mother as *paternal* relates to the father. *Sororal* relates to the sister as *fraternal* relates to the brother.

97. (A) A group that is *homogeneous* is alike, not *dissimilar*. A person who is *sanguine* is optimistic, not *pessimistic*.

98. (B) To *terminate* is to end, whereas to *found* is to start up. To *exterminate* is to kill, whereas to *revive* is to bring back to life.

99. (C) The opposite of *veritable* (true) is *false*. The opposite of *venerable* (respected) is *disreputable*.

100. (C) If an event is *remarkable*, it is not *mundane*, or ordinary. If an animal is *feral*, or wild, it is not *domesticated*.

Chapter 3: Degree Analogies

101. (A) To be *obsequious* is to be extremely *polite*, to the point of a negative connotation. To be *spineless* is to be extremely *lenient*, again with a negative connotation.

102. (A) If you are *obese*, you are more than *chubby*. If you are *uncontrollable*, you are more than *disruptive*.

103. (C) If something *implodes*, it *collapses* violently. In a similar vein, to *importune* is to make a *request* in the most dramatic of ways.

104. (C) A *forgery* is a *replica* taken to extremes for nefarious purposes. *Mortification* is extreme *chagrin*, or embarrassment.

105. (A) To *hurl* is to *throw* hard; to *flop* is to *sit* hard.

106. (B) To be *manic* is to be very *busy*. To be *deafening* is to be very *noisy*.

107. (B) If you are very *fearful*, you are *terrified*. If you are very *surprised*, you are *astounded*.

108. (C) If you really *want* something, you *crave* it. If you really *like* someone, you *worship* him or her.

109. (D) A *magnum* is a very large *bottle*, and a *salver* is a large *plate* or tray.

110. (A) *Extremely* is greater than *very*, and *rarely* is greater than *intermittently*.

111. (D) To be *indestructible* is to be very *durable*. To be *wily* is to be very *clever*.

112. (A) If you are more than a little *keen* on a topic, one might say you were *fanatical*. If you were more than a little *interested* in some reading material, one might say you were *engrossed* in it.

113. (D) A *vial* is a small container; a *vat* is a large container. A *filament* is a small thread; a *rope* is a large thread.

114. (B) If you *harangue* someone, you *lecture* him or her aggressively. If you *hoard* something, you *store* it secretly or fanatically.

115. (D) The analogy here is A is to C as B is to D. Someone who is very *mischievous* may be *wicked* while someone who is very *self-indulgent* may be *hedonistic*.

116. (B) An *aria* may be considered a very fancy *melody*, and a *prom* may be considered a very fancy *dance*.

117. (C) A *misdemeanor* is a lesser crime than a *felony*. *Petit larceny* is a lesser crime than *grand larceny*.

118. (D) A *shove* is a sharp *push*. A *yank* is a sharp *pull*.

119. (A) To *protect* strongly is to *guard*. To *collect* significantly is to *stockpile*.

120. (C) To *prod* with vigor is to *stab*. To *disobey* with vigor is to *flout*.

121. (A) If you *tinge* something, you add a bit of color or liquid to it. If you *saturate* something, you drench it. Something that is *sentimental* is a bit emotional. Something that is *maudlin* is over the top.

122. (A) Great *concern* may be *anxiety*. Great *imagination* may be *delusion*.

123. (A) To be very *unwieldy* is to be *cumbersome*. To be very *sober*, or serious, is to be *grim*.

124. (B) To *tread* heavily is to *stomp*. To *strike* heavily is to *clobber*.

125. (B) If you are very *disgruntled*, or displeased, you may be *livid*. If you are very *restless*, or on edge, you may be *frantic*.

126. (D) A *fad* taken too far might be a *mania*. *Enjoyment* taken too far might be *enthrallment*.

127. (D) A huge *wave* is a *tsunami*. A huge *hollow* is a *chasm*.

128. (A) A *throng* is a dense *group*, and a *jungle* is a dense *woodland*.

129. (D) To *spew* is to *emit* strongly, and to *outlaw* is to *forbid* strongly.

130. (A) An extreme *dribble* might be a *slobber*, and an extreme form of to *follow* might be to *stalk*.

131. (A) If you are very *delicate*, you might be considered *feeble*. If you are very *fit*, you might be considered *brawny*.

132. (C) To be overly *fond* is to be *doting*. To be overly *harmful* is to be *destructive*.

133. (D) If you are very *untidy*, you may be *slovenly*. If you are very *full*, you may be *bursting*.

134. (C) A very *mellow* tone may be called *plummy*, and a very *high-pitched* tone may be called *piercing*.

135. (D) A *precipice* is a very steep *bluff*, and a *cataract* is a very large *waterfall*.

136. (D) If you are very *optimistic* about an occurrence, you might be *triumphant*. If you are very *lukewarm* on a subject, you might be *apathetic*.

137. (D) An action that is very *abrupt* might be considered *rude*. A discussion that is very *long* might be considered *protracted*.

138. (D) If you *approved* enormously of a plan, you might *bless* it. If you *disapproved* enormously, you might *censure*, or condemn, it.

139. (C) To *bind* is to *connect* tightly, and to *impel*, or force, is to *influence* strongly.

140. (A) A very *harmful* substance may be *toxic*, and a very *disapproving* person may be *hostile*.

141. (A) Someone who is very *needy* may be *destitute*. Something that is very *minor* may be *inconsequential*.

142. (D) To *thrive* is to *achieve* greatly. To *agonize* is to *worry* greatly.

143. (A) To be extremely *direct* is to be *undeviating*. To be extremely *brief* is to be *brusque*.

144. (B) A negative connotation of *tame* is *subjugate*. A negative connotation of *use* is *squander*.

145. (A) A *march* that is out of control is a *stampede*. A *force* that is out of control is a *juggernaut*.

146. (D) A *hovel* is an extremely horrible *shack*. *Slavery* is an extremely horrible form of *repression*.

147. (C) To *accede* completely is to *surrender*. To *wane* completely is to *disappear*.

148. (A) A very *particular* person may be described as *finicky*. A very *unnatural* act may be described as *perverted*.

149. (D) If you *neglect* someone entirely, you *abandon* him or her. If you *pester* someone unmercifully, you *harass* him or her.

150. (C) An *arteriole* is the tiniest *artery*. Arterioles connect arteries with capillaries. A *venule* is the tiniest *vein*. Venules connect veins with capillaries.

Chapter 4: Affix Analogies

151. (D) The suffix *-er* means "one who," as in *worker* or *dancer*. The suffix *-ful* means "full of," as in *beautiful* or *joyful*.

152. (B) The prefix *quasi-* means "somewhat," as in *quasi-formal*. The prefix *hemi-* means "half," as in *hemisphere*.

153. (A) To *abstain* or *abandon* is to move away from something or someone; to *adhere* or *adopt* is to move toward something or someone.

154. (D) *Mega-* is a prefix that refers to great size, as in *megaphone* or *megaton*.

155. (C) *Xer* means "dry," as in *xeric*. *Xyl* means "wooden," as in *xylem* or *xylophone*.

156. (A) Here, A is to C as B is to D. *Verb* is a root meaning "word," and *vert* is a root meaning "turn," as in *invert* or *vertex* (turning point).

157. (A) *Omni-* is a prefix that means "all," as in *omnivorous*. *Poly-* is a prefix that means "many," as in *polygamous*.

158. (B) The prefix *kilo-*, as in *kilogram*, means "thousand." The prefix *hecto-*, as in *hectare*, means "hundred."

159. (D) *Poli*, as in *metropolitan*, means "city." *Peri*, as in *perimeter*, means "around."

160. (A) Dogs are often named Fido because they are faithful friends. Other words with the root *fid* include *fidelity* and *infidel*.

161. (B) These medical roots appear in words such as *cerebral* and *cranium*.

162. (D) The prefix *iso-* means "equal," as in *isotope*. The prefix *ethno-* means "people," as in *ethnic*.

163. (C) The suffix *-ist* changes a noun into another noun, as in *pianist* or *Marxist*. The suffix *-ish* changes a noun into an adjective, as in *foolish* or *fiendish*.

164. (A) Here, A is to C as B is to D. *Leuko* means "white," as in *leukemia*, a disease of the colorless cells in the lymph and blood. *Lacto* means "milk," as in *lactation*.

165. (D) *Sect* mean "to cut," as in *dissect* or *section*. *Spect* means "to look," as in *inspect* or *spectacle*.

166. (B) The prefix *telo-*, as in *telophase*, means "end." The prefix *tele-*, as in *telescope*, means "distant."

167. (C) *Octa-* is a Greek prefix that means "eight," as in *octagon*. *Dodeca-* is a Greek prefix that means "12"; a *dodecagon* has 12 sides.

168. (B) Think of words you know that contain each root. For example, a *hypodermic* injects *below* the skin. *Homophones* are words that sound the *same*.

169. (D) The prefix *mis-* means "wrong," as in *misspoke*. The prefix *im-* means "not," as in *impossible*.

170. (A) The root *dict*, as in *dictation*, means "to speak." The root *duct*, as in *conductor*, means "to lead."

171. (D) To be *superior* is to be above something or someone. *Trans-* means "across," as in *transfer*, *transmit*, *transport*, and so on.

172. (C) *Chron* is a root that refers to time, as in *chronological*. *Dyna* is a root that refers to power, as in *dynamic*.

173. (A) A *bibliophile* loves books, and a *philanthropist* loves mankind. A *misanthrope*, on the other hand, hates mankind.

174. (A) Think of words that have the given suffixes. *Powerful* and *joyful* mean "full of power" and "full of joy." *Reality* and *clarity* mean the "state of being real" and the "state of being clear."

175. (D) The prefix *micro-* means "millionth," as in *microgram*. The prefix *nano-* means "billionth," as in *nanometer*.

176. (B) *Multi* means "many," as in *multicolored*. *Ambi* means "both," as in *ambidextrous*.

177. (A) The analogy here is A is to C as B is to D. *Circumference* means "the distance around." *Contradict* means "to speak against."

178. (C) *Tri-* is a prefix meaning "three." *Sept-* is a prefix meaning "seven." It is easy to get confused if you think about the months of the year—on our current calendar, September is the ninth month, and October is the tenth. But in the early Roman calendar, there were just 10 months in all, and September was the seventh.

179. (B) *Frag*, as in *fragment*, means "break." *Flux*, as in *influx*, means "flow."

180. (A) *Acri* means "sour" or "bitter," as in *acrid* or *acrimony*. *Agri* means "field" or "soil," as in *agriculture*.

181. (A) The prefix *ultra-*, as in *ultraconservative*, means "on the far side of," or "extremely." The prefix *ultima-*, as in *ultimatum*, means "last."

182. (C) These roots are often found in mathematics. A *tetrahedron* is a figure with four faces. An *ennead* is a set of nine.

183. (A) *Counter* means "against," as in *counteract*. *Com* means "with," as in *companion*.

184. (C) The root *ped* refers to a foot, as in *pedal* or *pedestrian*. The root *pedo* refers to a child, as in *pediatrics* or *pedophile*.

185. (B) *Nom* means "name," as in *nominative*. *Neur* means "nerve," as in *neurology*.

186. (A) The root *infra-*, as in *infrastructure*, means "beneath." The root *intra-*, as in *intramural*, means "within."

187. (A) *Phlegma* is a medical root that refers to *inflammation*. *Pneumo*, as in *pneumonia*, is a root that refers to *breath*.

188. (C) The root *rupt*, as in *interrupt* or *erupt*, means "break." The root *phage*, which you may recall from *bacteriophages* in biology class, means "eat."

189. (D) *Veri*, as in *veracity* or *verify*, means "true." *Vita*, as in *vitality* or *revitalize*, means "alive."

190. (B) The suffix *–ly* usually changes adjectives to adverbs, as in *strange* to *strangely*. The suffix *–ize* usually changes nouns to verbs, as in *critic* to *criticize*.

191. (D) These unusual suffixes are frequently used in medicine. For example, dextrocardia is a defect in which the heart points toward the *right* side of the body. Sinistrocular people use their *left* eye as their dominant eye.

192. (D) The prefix *gastro-*, as in *gastric ulcer*, refers to the *stomach*. The prefix *hepato-*, as in *hepatic artery*, refers to the *liver*.

193. (B) *-Lepsy*, as in *narcolepsy* or *epilepsy*, refers to a kind of *attack*. *–Lysis* means "destruction," as in *paralysis*, or "breakdown," as in *analysis*.

194. (C) *Graph* means "to write," as in *autograph* or *graphic*. *Gress* means "to walk," as in *progress* or *digress*.

195. (B) *Litho-* is a prefix meaning "stone," as in *lithograph* or *monolith*. *Lipo-* is a prefix meaning "fat," as in *lipid* or *liposuction*.

196. (B) *Voc*, as in *vocal* or *invocation*, means "call." *Vac*, as in *vacuum* or *vacate*, means "empty."

197. (C) *Lum* is a root meaning "light," as in *illuminate*. *Helio* is a root meaning "sun," as in *heliocentric*.

198. (D) The prefix *hemo-*, as in *hemoglobin*, means "blood." The prefix *hemi-*, as in *hemisphere*, means "half."

199. (C) *Aqu* should be recognizable as a root that means "water," and if you think of words containing *ignis*—*ignite*, *igneous*—the connection to *fire* should be clear.

200. (A) *Peristalsis* is the *contraction* of muscles in the alimentary canal and intestine. *Stasis* is a state of equilibrium, inactivity, or *stopping*, as in *homeostasis*.

Chapter 5: Classification Analogies

201. (A) Just as *appliqué* is a particular form of *stitchery*, *intaglio* is a particular form of *printmaking*.

202. (C) A *coach* is one form of *conveyance*, or transport; a *roach* (cockroach) is one form of *insect*.

203. (C) The name *Ada* is a *palindrome* (a word that is spelled the same way backward and forward). The sound *arf* is an example of *onomatopoeia*, a word that imitates the sound it names.

204. (A) A *Weimeraner* is one breed of *dog*, as a *Percheron* is one breed of *horse*. Manx (B) are cats, Wyandottes (C) are chickens, and Pomeranians (D) are dogs.

205. (D) *Caffeine* is a popular and legal *stimulant*, and *alcohol* is a popular and legal *depressant*.

206. (B) A *novella* is a short piece of fiction—longer than a short story, but shorter than a *novel*. Choices A, C, and D are all lengthy novels.

207. (A) A *trapezoid* is one kind of *quadrilateral*, or four-sided figure. A *square* is one kind of *rectangle*, or four-sided figure with four right angles.

208. (D) A *puffin* is a northern *seabird*. A *puffball* is a ball-shaped *fungus*.

209. (B) *Qolsharif* is a *mosque* in India, and *Notre Dame* is a *cathedral* in Paris. Choice A is a synagogue, choice C is a temple, and choice D is a mission.

210. (A) A *fresco* is a *painting* on plaster. An *amphora* is *pottery*, a clay jug.

211. (B) The *Studebaker* was a brand of *automobile*, as *Old Town* was a brand of *canoe*.

212. (D) *Glucose* is one form of *sugar*, and *ethanol*, sometimes used as fuel, is one form of *alcohol*.

213. (B) Lake *Huron* is one of the five *Great Lakes*; the others are Michigan, Erie, Superior, and Ontario. *Cayuga* Lake is one of the five *Finger Lakes* in upstate New York; the others are Canandaigua, Keuka, Seneca, and Owasco.

214. (D) The *Dakota* people are a subset of the *Sioux* Nation, and the *Hopi* people are a subset of the *Pueblo*.

215. (C) The only *woodwind* in the list of choices is the *saxophone*; the others are all *brass* instruments.

216. (C) The word *kindly* is an *adverb*, a word that modifies a verb, adjective, or another adverb. The word *kindness* is a *noun*, a word that names a person, place, thing, or idea.

217. (C) *Boron* is an *element*, atomic number 5 on the Periodic Table of Elements. *Borax* is a *compound* made up primarily of sodium and boron.

218. (A) Ancient *Sparta* was an example of a *hegemony*—government through threat of force of one state over others. The *United Arab Republic* was an example of a *confederation*—a union of partly or mostly self-governing states.

219. (B) An *eel* is a *bony* fish, as are trout, coelacanths, and sturgeon. A *shark* is a *cartilaginous* fish—its skeleton is made of cartilage rather than bone. Its cousins are rays and skates.

220. (D) *Elizabeth I* (1533–1603) was a scion of the House of *Tudor*. *Elizabeth II* (b. 1926) is a scion of the House of *Windsor*.

221. (D) Of the books listed, only *Malachi* is found in the *Old Testament*. The others appear in the *New Testament*.

222. (B) An *organic* compound is typically one that contains carbon and is necessary for life. Pure carbon, such as diamond, is considered *inorganic*. Salt and water may be necessary for life, but they do not contain carbon.

223. (B) *"If I Had a Hammer"* is a *folk song* by Pete Seeger and Lee Hays. *"Un bel di, vedremo"* is an *aria* sung by Butterfly in Puccini's *Madama Butterfly*.

224. (A) There are 59 *national parks* in the United States; *Acadia* is a park in Maine. There are 155 *national forests* in the United States; *Olympia* is a forest in Washington State. The other three choices are national parks.

225. (C) The *Gulf* of *Aqaba* lies along the eastern shore of the Sinai Peninsula. The *Bay* of *Bengal* lies along the eastern shore of India.

226. (C) *Kronos* was one of the *Titans*, the primordial giant gods in Greek mythology. *Zeus* was one of the *Olympians*, the gods who inhabited Mount Olympus.

227. (C) During World War II, *Germany* and its supporters were called the *Axis*. *Great Britain* and its supporters were called the *Allies*.

228. (D) *"30 Rock"* was a popular TV situation comedy, or *sitcom*. It ran for seven years, from 2006 to 2013. *"General Hospital,"* which first aired in 1963, is the longest-running *soap opera* on American television.

229. (D) The *Niger* is a *river* in Africa, and the *Suez* is a *canal* in Africa. The other choices are all rivers.

230. (A) Luciano *Pavarotti* was a famous Italian *tenor*, and Renata *Scotto* is a famous Italian *soprano*. José Carreras and Placido Domingo are tenors, and Marian Anderson was a contralto.

231. (B) A *ram* is a male *ovine*, or sheep. A *tom* is a male *feline*, or cat.

232. (A) *Gymnosperms* such as *pine* trees have no flowers to protect their seeds. *Angiosperms* such as *oak* trees have seed-bearing flowers.

233. (B) The *biathlon*, which features cross-country skiing and rifle shooting, is part of the *Winter Olympics*. The other sports are all events in the *Summer Olympics*.

234. (A) A *baleen whale* is one kind of whale, and a *dogfish shark* is one kind of shark.

235. (B) *Carrots* are an example of a vegetable whose *roots* we eat. *Onions* are an example of a vegetable whose *bulbs* we eat.

236. (A) A *shoat* is a baby *pig*. A *cygnet* is a baby *swan*.

237. (D) *Pamela*, a 1742 novel by Samuel Richardson, is *epistolary*; it is written in the form of letters. *Tom Jones*, a 1749 novel by Henry Fielding, is *picaresque*; it relates the adventures of a roguish hero from his boyhood through adulthood.

238. (D) *Ecru* is a particular shade of *beige*. *Chartreuse* is a particular shade of *green*.

239. (A) *Barley* is a type of *grain*, and the whey cheese called *ricotta* is a *dairy* product.

240. (C) The *Germanic* languages are a subset of *Indo-European* languages. The *Semitic* languages are a subset of the *Afro-Asiatic* languages.

241. (B) Jean *Courbet* was a leader of the French Realist movement in painting. Pierre-Auguste *Renoir* was a leader of the French Impressionist movement.

242. (A) All of the animals listed are *amphibians,* except the *turtle,* which is a *reptile.*

243. (B) *Worsted* is one kind of *wool* cloth. *Shantung* is one kind of *silk* cloth.

244. (C) *Samoan* is classified as one of the *Polynesian* languages. *Cantonese* is one of the *Chinese* languages.

245. (C) *Homeland Security* is part of the *executive* branch of government, as are the National Security Council (B) and the Department of Commerce (D). The Sentencing Commission (A) is part of the judicial branch. The *Library of Congress,* as its name suggests, is part of the *legislative* branch.

246. (D) *Jack* is the name for a male *donkey. Bull* is the name for a male *alligator.*

247. (A) Canada has three territories and 10 provinces. *Yukon* is a *territory,* and *Manitoba* is a *province.* The other choices are *provinces* (C and D) and a city (B).

248. (C) A *snake* has a backbone and is thus a *vertebrate.* A *scorpion* has an outer shell rather than a backbone and is thus an *invertebrate.*

249. (A) *Thalia* was one of the three *Graces,* representing good cheer. (There was a Muse named Thalia as well.) *Clotho* was one of the three *Fates,* the one responsible for spinning the thread of human life.

250. (C) *Corn* is a *monocot* plant; its seeds have only one section (one seed leaf, or cotyledon). All of the other plants listed are *dicots*; their seeds have two sections.

Chapter 6: Part/Whole Analogies

251. (C) *New York* is subdivided into *counties,* but the same kind of governmental division is called a *parish* in *Louisiana.*

252. (B) *Majorca* is a Mediterranean island owned by *Spain. Corsica* is a Mediterranean island owned by *France.*

253. (C) The *IRS* (Internal Revenue Service) and *OSHA* (Occupational Safety and Health Administration) are governmental departments within the *Treasury* Department and *Labor* Department, respectively.

254. (A) *Wingers* are the fast scorers on a *rugby* team, and *forwards* are the fast scorers on a *hockey* team.

255. (A) A *deer* or rabbit has a short, erect tail called a *scut*. A *monkey*, on the other hand, has a long, *prehensile tail*.

256. (B) The part of a *spoon* that holds food is the *bowl*, and the part of a *fork* that spears food is the *tine*.

257. (D) An *opera* is divided into *acts*, and a *symphony* is divided into *movements*.

258. (D) The *fibula* and *tibia* are the outer and inner leg bones. The *radius* and *ulna* are the outer and inner arm bones.

259. (C) A *cymbal* is part of the *percussion* section as a *horn* is part of the *wind* section of an orchestra or band.

260. (D) The analogy here is A is to C as B is to D. A *cup* is part of a *pint*; an *inch* is part of a *foot*.

261. (B) The driver of a *tugboat* works in the *wheelhouse*, and the driver of a *jet* works in the *cockpit*.

262. (A) A *faun* is a mythical creature that is part man and part *goat*. A *harpy* is a mythical creature that is part woman and part *bird*.

263. (B) The color *blue* is one part of *purple* (the other is red). The color *yellow* is one part of *orange* (again, the other is red).

264. (D) *Japan* is divided into governmental regions called *prefectures*. *Switzerland* is divided into governmental regions called *cantons*.

265. (A) The *frame* of a *bicycle* defines its structure much as the *hull* of a *canoe* defines its structure.

266. (D) Both the *arch* and the *toe* are part of a foot. Both the *palm* and the *thumb* are part of a hand.

267. (B) *Tesserae* are the little tiles used to make a *mosaic*. *Pixels* are the smallest "picture elements" of a *digital photo*.

268. (A) *Sumatra* is an island that is part of the archipelago of *Indonesia*. *Honshu* is an island that is part of the archipelago of *Japan*.

269. (D) *France* is a member of the European Union, or *EU. Russia* is a member of the United Nations, or *UN*.

270. (B) A *cube's* faces are *squares*, and most or all of a *pyramid's* faces are *triangles*.

271. (A) *Avarice* and *envy* are two of the seven sins. *Eucharist* and *penance* are two of the seven sacraments.

272. (A) Ammunition is inserted into the *chamber* of a *revolver* or the *bore* of a *cannon*.

273. (C) The *cork* is the part of a *wine bottle* that keeps its contents inside. The *sphincter* is the part of the *stomach* that keeps its contents inside.

274. (B) The analogy here is A is to C as B is to D. A *college* may be one part of a *university*. A *chamber* may be one part of a *parliament*.

275. (C) During the Civil War, *Ohio* was a blue state, or part of the *Union*, and *Alabama* as well as the other states listed in the choices were gray states, or part of the *Confederacy*.

276. (C) The *cap* is the sometimes edible top part of a *mushroom*. The *spear* is the stalk and tip of the *asparagus* plant.

277. (D) A long string of *islands* is called an *atoll*. A long string of *mountains* is called a *range*.

278. (D) A *mantel* is a horizontal structure over a *fireplace*. A *lintel* is a horizontal structure over a *doorway*.

279. (C) Whereas a *carrot* and other green plants get nutrients from the soil via roots and *root hairs*, a *liverwort* and some other land plants get their nutrients through *rhizoids*.

280. (D) The analogy here is A is to C as B is to D. A *book* opens and closes along its *spine*, and a *hinge* opens and closes along its *pin*.

281. (B) One ingredient of *brass* is *copper*. One ingredient of *steel* is *iron*.

282. (A) The modern *pentathlon* is an athletic contest that features five events—running, swimming, horseback riding, *fencing*, and pistol shooting. A *decathlon* is an athletic contest that features 10 track-and-field events, including *pole vaulting*.

283. (D) *Borscht* is a Ukrainian soup that has a *beetroot* base. *Mulligatawny* is an Anglo-Indian soup that has a *curry* base.

284. (B) The *crossbar* is a horizontal structure that helps to hold and steady an *easel*. The *boom* is a horizontal structure that helps to hold and steady a *sail*.

285. (A) *Constantinople* was the capital of the *Ottoman Empire*. *Prague* was one of several capitals of the *Holy Roman Empire*.

286. (A) The gelatinous material that fills the *eye* is called the *vitreous humor*. The gelatinous material that lines the *spinal cord* is called *gray matter*.

287. (A) *Grasshoppers* and other insects breathe through slits called *spiracles*. *Fish* breathe through slits called *gills*.

288. (C) The *Mennonites* are a sect of the *Anabaptists*, a group of Protestants who believe in rebaptizing new members (and not baptizing infants). The *Sunni* are a sect of *Muslims* who hold that the true succession of Muslim leadership comes not from Muhammad's son-in-law Ali, but rather from the original four Caliphs.

289. (A) One part of the capital letter *A* is its *bar*. One part of the capital letter *Q* is its *tail*.

290. (B) The *caudate lobe* is part of the *liver*, and the *parietal lobe* is part of the *cerebrum*.

291. (B) In an army, a *corps* holds two or more *divisions*, and a *regiment* holds two or more *battalions*.

292. (C) Francis *Beaumont* and John *Fletcher* were Elizabethan dramatists and collaborators. W. S. *Gilbert* and Arthur *Sullivan* collaborated on a number of light operas in the late nineteenth century.

293. (D) Just as a *sentence* may be part of a *paragraph*, so a *line* may be part of a *stanza*.

294. (B) A group of *crows* is called a *murder*. A group of *badgers* is called a *sett*.

295. (A) *Wallpaper* may be the background on a *computer screen*, and the *field* is the background on a *coat of arms*.

296. (A) A *quatrain* is typically part of a *ballad*. A *sonata* is typically part of a *symphony*.

297. (C) A *serial*, as on television, is made up of *episodes*. A *cereal* grain has three parts, one of which is *bran*.

298. (D) A *phalanx* is any of the bones in a *finger* or toe. The *mandible* is the lower bone of the *jaw*.

299. (B) There are eight *bits* in a *byte* (a unit of measure of computer memory). There are eight *pints* in a *gallon*.

300. (B) The *salivary glands* are in the *mouth*. The *gastric glands* are in the *stomach*.

Chapter 7: Conversion Analogies

301. (D) Although the two numbers 4 and 5 are sequential, that relationship does not hold in the analogy as presented. Looking at the relationship between 4 and 64, you should notice that $64 = 4^3$ and similarly, $125 = 5^3$.

302. (A) *Mercury* is the Roman name for the Greek god *Hermes*, and *Neptune* is the Roman name for the Greek god *Poseidon*.

303. (C) *Cu* is the atomic symbol for the element *copper*. *Fe* (from the Latin word *ferrum*) is the atomic symbol for the element *iron*.

304. (C) The country of *Namibia* was once known as *South-West Africa*, and the country of *Ethiopia* was once known as *Abyssinia*.

305. (A) *Aurora* and *Pluto* are the Roman names for the Greek gods *Eos* and *Hades*.

306. (C) The South American revolutionary *Ernesto Guevara* was given the nickname *Che*. The western lawman and gunfighter *James Butler Hickok* was given the nickname *Wild Bill*.

307. (C) The fractions 2/5 and 5/2 are reciprocals; in other words, $2/5 \times 5/2 = 1$. The fractions 3/7 and 7/3 are also reciprocals.

308. (C) The words *map* and *amp* contain the same letters in mixed order, as do the words *diet* and *tide*.

309. (D) Many world cities have changed names as the cultures surrounding them changed. *Aix La Chappelle* is on the border of France and Germany and now goes by its German name, *Aachen*. *Bombay* was a European name for the city now called *Mumbai*.

310. (D) Both 10/100 and 40/400 name the same fraction.

311. (A) *Tokyo*, Japan, was called *Edo* until 1868. *Ho Chi Minh City*, Vietnam, was called *Saigon* until 1976.

312. (B) Changing the letter *a* to *o* changes *adapted* to *adopted*. The same change makes *decay* into *decoy*.

313. (C) President William Henry *Harrison* became known as *Tippecanoe* following his success in the Battle of Tippecanoe when he was military governor of the territory of Indiana. President Dwight David *Eisenhower* was known as *Ike* from boyhood. Both nicknames figured in their presidential campaigns: "Tippecanoe and Tyler Too" and "I Like Ike" are among the most famous of campaign slogans.

314. (B) Think: A is to C as B is to D. The fraction 3/4 renames the decimal 0.75. The fraction 4/5 renames the decimal 0.80.

315. (D) Adding an *e* to *nigh* changes both the word and the pronunciation. Adding an *e* to *size* does the same thing.

316. (B) The island in the South China Sea once known as *Formosa* is now called *Taiwan*. The island in the Indian Ocean once called *Ceylon* is now called *Sri Lanka*.

317. (A) *Natty Bumppo* was the unlikely name of the character known as the *Deerslayer* in James Fenimore Cooper's book by that name. *Christopher Newman* was the character known as the *American* in Henry James's book by that name.

318. (C) *Bacteria* is plural; *bacterium* is singular. *Data* is plural; *datum* is singular.

319. (B) In each pair of words, the middle consonant is doubled.

320. (B) *Tempi* is the plural form of *tempo*. *Choruses* is the plural form of *chorus*.

321. (A) On the Celsius scale, 100 is the boiling point of water, and 0 is the freezing point of water. On the Fahrenheit scale, 212 is the boiling point of water, and 32 is the freezing point of water.

322. (A) *Harvard* teams are the *Crimson*. *Yale* teams are the *Bulldogs*.

323. (D) Each pair of words features a change in vowel from *u* to *a*.

324. (A) Even in the United States, certain cities have changed names over time. Examples are the New York towns of *Sleepy Hollow* and *Ossining*.

325. (D) The two pairs of words are homophones—words that sound alike but are spelled differently and have different meanings.

326. (B) A resident of *Ohio* may be referred to as a *Buckeye*. A resident of *Iowa* may be referred to as a *Hawkeye*.

327. (C) The symbols shown stand for *copyright* and *trademark*.

328. (C) The best parallel is one in which the letter *f* is added at the beginning of the word.

329. (C) *Peking* was an Anglicization of the Chinese name for that city. It is now rendered as *Beijing*, which is closer to the real pronunciation. *Istanbul* has had many names, from Byzantium through *Constantinople*, including Islambol.

330. (A) 25/75 is equivalent to 1/3, as is 30/90.

331. (A) *Zeus* is the Greek name for the god known as *Jupiter* by the Romans. *Cronus* (or Kronos) is the Greek name for the Titan known as *Saturn* by the Romans.

332. (B) The Central American country of *Belize* was formerly known as *British Honduras*. The South American country of *Guyana* was formerly known as *British Guiana*.

333. (B) The Greek letters shown are *delta* and *gamma*.

334. (B) *York* was an earlier name for *Toronto*, and *Ville-Marie* was an earlier name for the French-speaking city, *Montreal*.

335. (C) You can look at this analogy either as A is to B as C is to D, in which case the fraction formed by the numbers is equivalent to 2/3, or as A is to C as B is to D, in which case the fraction formed is equivalent to 1/2. Either way, the answer is 66.

336. (A) For modernizing Prussia, *Frederick II* was known as *the Great*. The Russian czar *Ivan IV* was known as *the Terrible*.

337. (D) Doubling the *r* in *fury* produces *furry*. Doubling the *l* in *holy* produces *holly*.

338. (A) Many of Beethoven's symphonies have nicknames; *Beethoven's Third* is called *Eroica* and *Beethoven's Sixth* is called *Pastoral.*

339. (A) President *Martin Van Buren* gained his nickname, *Old Kinderhook*, due to his hometown of Kinderhook, NY. President *Zachary Taylor* earned his nickname, *Old Rough and Ready,* due to his military leadership.

340. (A) *French Sudan* became *Mali* upon independence in 1960. *Rhodesia* became *Zimbabwe* upon independence in 1980.

341. (C) *Juno* is the Roman name for the Greek goddess *Hera. Bacchus* is the Roman name for the Greek god *Dionysus.*

342. (C) 0.016 is the decimal equivalent of 1/64, and 0.125 is the decimal equivalent of 1/8.

343. (D) Prior to partition, the nation of *Bangladesh* was *East Pakistan. Myanmar* is the local name for the nation still called *Burma* by the United States and the United Kingdom.

344. (B) The first symbol is the Greek letter *alpha.* The second is the Greek letter *theta.*

345. (C) *USC* teams are the *Trojans*, and *UCLA* teams are the *Bruins.*

346. (D) The plural of *louse* is *lice;* the plural of *bison* is *bison.*

347. (A) Actress *Marilyn Monroe* was born *Norma Jean Baker,* and actress/singer *Judy Garland* was born *Frances Gumm.* The other choices are birth names for Judy Holliday (B), Shirley MacLaine (C), and Barbara Stanwyck (D).

348. (C) *Venus* is the Roman name for the Greek goddess *Aphrodite. Mars* is the Roman name for the Greek god *Ares.*

349. (C) King *Richard I* was known as Richard *the Lionhearted.* King *Ethelred II* was known as Ethelred *the Unready,* because of his young age at succession (only 10) and his lack of success at stemming Scandinavian invasions.

350. (B) The first symbol is called an *asterisk.* The dots in a series are known as *ellipses.*

Chapter 8: Characteristic Analogies

351. (C) The grasslands of *North America* are known as *prairies*, and those of *South America* are known as *pampas*.

352. (B) In Greek mythology, both *Clio* and *Urania* were muses, and each had a special assignment. Clio's was *history*, and Urania's was *astronomy*.

353. (D) Whereas the *Gospels* of Mark, Matthew, Luke, and John are *biographies* of Christ, the Book of *Revelation* is a *prophecy* of the future.

354. (C) The *University of Virginia* is located in *Charlottesville*, and the *University of Pennsylvania* is in *Philadelphia*.

355. (B) *Skeletal* muscle is *voluntary*; the animal controls its contractions consciously. *Cardiac* muscle is *involuntary*; contractions are outside of the animal's conscious control.

356. (A) The main ingredient of a *mornay* sauce is *cheese*. The main ingredient of a *béchamel* sauce is a *roux*, a mixture of flour and fat, usually butter.

357. (B) *Spanish* is the principal language of *Cuba*, and *French* is the principal language of *Haiti*.

358. (A) A *peridot* is a pale *green* gemstone. A *garnet* is a deep *red* gemstone.

359. (C) A *king* runs a *monarchy*, but the *wealthy* elite run a *plutocracy*.

360. (D) The *Prado* is an art museum in *Madrid*, and the *Tate* is an art museum in *London*. The other museums listed are in St. Petersburg, Russia; Davos, Switzerland; and Bath, England.

361. (B) The biblical king *Solomon* was known for his *wisdom*, and the biblical judge *Samson* was known for his *strength*.

362. (C) Everyone is familiar with the date of the *Declaration of Independence*. Not so familiar is 1848, the date of the signing of Elizabeth Cady Stanton's *Seneca Falls Declaration*, which declared women equal to men.

363. (B) David *Farragut* was an admiral in the US *Navy* during the Civil War. William Tecumseh *Sherman* was a general in the US *Army* during the Civil War.

364. (D) Dwight *Eisenhower* was born in *Texas*. Richard *Nixon* was born in *California*. Although Ronald Reagan (B) lived in California and served as governor there, he was born in Illinois.

365. (D) A *eukaryotic* cell has a nucleus. Most living things, including *fish*, are eukaryotes. A *prokaryotic* cell has no nucleus. Prokaryotes are either *bacteria* or archaea.

366. (C) The Greek marble statue known as Winged Victory is housed at the Louvre in *Paris*, France, just as the Renaissance statue of *David* is now located in the Accademia Gallery in *Florence*, Italy.

367. (C) *Chlorophyll* gives *spinach* its green color. *Carotenoid* gives *carrots* their orange color.

368. (A) *OCD*, or obsessive-compulsive disorder, is a neurosis marked by *anxiety*. *Schizophrenia* is a psychosis often marked by *hallucinations*.

369. (A) *Cumulus* clouds are *puffy* and white. *Cirrus* clouds are *wispy* and gray.

370. (C) Lack of *iodine* can cause the swelling of the thyroid known as a *goiter*. Lack of *vitamin C* can lead to the deficiency disease called *scurvy*.

371. (D) *Vodka* is liquor traditionally made from *potatoes*. *Rum* is liquor traditionally made from *molasses*.

372. (A) *Horses* are *odd-toed*. They have one toe on each foot, as do burros (C) and zebras (D). *Giraffes*, cattle, sheep, goats, pigs, and deer (so-called "cloven-hoof" animals) are *even-toed*—they have hooves that are split into two toes apiece. A rhinoceros has three toes on each foot.

373. (A) A *concho* is a *silver* ornament used on belts or clothing. A *cornet* is a *brass* instrument.

374. (C) *DNA* is in a shape known as *helical*. *Maple leaves* are in a lobed shape known as *palmate*.

375. (C) The view of *Fort McHenry* during the Battle of Baltimore, fought during the *War of 1812*, inspired Francis Scott Key to write "The Star-Spangled Banner" in 1814. The battle at *Fort Sumter* in 1861 was the beginning of the *Civil War*.

376. (B) A *glider* is marked by its lack of a *motor*, and an *integrated circuit* is marked by its lack of *wires*.

377. (C) The *peso* is the currency of *Chile*. The *riyal* is the currency of *Saudi Arabia*.

378. (A) The elements known as *metals* are *malleable* (bendable) and conductive. Those known as *nonmetals* tend to be *brittle* and nonconductive.

379. (D) The rock known as *sandstone* is usually *tan* in color. The volcanic rock known as *basalt* is usually *black*.

380. (C) *Hatching* is a form of drawing characterized by making short, parallel or perpendicular *lines*. *Stippling* is a form of drawing characterized by making a pattern of small *dots*.

381. (A) *Karate* is a martial art from *Japan* that emphasizes striking movements. *Tai chi* is a martial art from *China* that emphasizes balance and slow, repetitive movements.

382. (C) *Doldrums* are characterized by a lack of *wind*. A *stalemate*, as in a battle or game of chess, is characterized by a lack of *movement*.

383. (B) In the *Wonderful Wizard of Oz*, the character of the *Lion* believes that he lacks *courage*, and the *Tin Man* believes that he lacks a heart, or *compassion*.

384. (A) *Alpine*, downhill, and slalom skiing all take place on *fixed-heel* skis. *Free-heel* skis are used for cross-country, or *Nordic*, skiing.

385. (A) *St. Peter's Basilica* has a large dome with ribs, known as an *umbrella dome*. The pinched-off style known as the *onion dome* is typical of Russian architecture, as in St. Basil's, and Mughal architecture, as in the *Taj Mahal*.

386. (D) *Ellesmere* is a large island in the *Arctic Ocean*, and *Sumatra* is a large island in the *Indian Ocean*.

387. (C) The god *Mercury*, messenger to the gods, was known for his *speed*. The goddess *Venus* was known for her *beauty*.

388. (A) The *mambo* is an Afro-Cuban dance in 4/4 time. The *tango* is an Argentinian dance, usually in 2/4 time.

389. (C) *Porcelain* is a fine china made from the soft, white clay called *kaolin*. A *tapestry* is a hanging form of textile art that is often made of *wool*.

390. (B) In stories and myths, *bulls* are typically *powerful*, and *coyotes* are *tricky*.

391. (C) The style of architecture known as *Neoclassical* is characterized by its *symmetrical* design. The style known as *Italianate* is characterized by flat, *blocky* shapes.

392. (A) *Tissue* is *translucent*; it allows some light to penetrate. *Wood* is *opaque*; it prevents light from penetrating.

393. (C) *Impetigo* is an infection of the *skin*. *Phlebitis* is the inflammation of a *vein*.

394. (C) Johann Sebastian *Bach* was a composer of the *Baroque* period (around 1600–1750). Ludwig van *Beethoven* was a composer of the *Classical* period (around 1750–1830).

395. (A) The skin plates known as *scales* on *snakes* are called *scutes* on *turtles* and alligators.

396. (D) The *Highlands* are a mountainous region of *Scotland*. The *steppes* are a plainlike region of *Russia*.

397. (C) *Hobnails*, found in old boots, were once made of *iron*. *Fingernails* are made of a protein called *keratin*.

398. (B) *Mecca*, in Saudi Arabia, is the birthplace of *Muhammad*. *Bethlehem*, on the West Bank in Israel, is the birthplace of *Jesus*.

399. (B) All of *India* is north of the equator, placing it in the *Northern Hemisphere*. The other countries named are south of the equator.

400. (D) A *mane* of fur around the neck is typical of a male *lion*. A bristly *beard* extending from the neck is typical of a male *turkey*.

Chapter 9: Sequence Analogies

401. (D) In the Bible, *Abraham* was the father of *Isaac*. In Greek mythology, *Zeus* was the father of *Apollo*.

402. (C) In singing voices, *contralto* is one step down in range from *mezzo-soprano*, and *bass* is one step down in range from *baritone*.

403. (A) When it is 7:00 Eastern Standard Time (*EST*), it is 4:00 Pacific Standard Time (*PST*).

404. (D) *Wilbur* and *Orville* were the Wright brothers; *Wilhelm* and *Jacob* were the Brothers Grimm.

405. (C) A *filly* is a young *mare*, or female horse. A *spat* is a young *oyster*.

406. (D) Multiple *rehearsals* may take place before a *performance* is ready. Multiple *prototypes* may be created before a *product* is ready.

407. (C) The month before *November* is *October*. The day before *Wednesday* is *Tuesday*.

408. (B) *Eric the Red* was the father of *Leif Ericsson*. *Henry VIII* was the father of *Elizabeth I*.

409. (B) As a *framework* may be the foundation for a *skyscraper*, a *charter* may be the underpinnings of a *government* or corporation.

410. (D) In the binary number system, or base 2, the order of numbers is 0, 1, 10, 11, 100, 101, 110, 111, and so on.

411. (C) The first and last major battles of the Civil War are usually considered to be the *Battle of Fort Sumter* and the *Battle of Columbus* (in Georgia), although many small skirmishes followed before the war was entirely over. In the American Revolution, the first and last major battles are usually considered to be the *Battle of Lexington and Concord* and the *Battle of Yorktown*. The other battles listed are from the Civil War (A), the War of 1812 (B), and the Spanish-American War (D).

412. (A) The four steps are the growth pattern of certain insects: from *egg* to *larva* to *pupa* to *imago*.

413. (D) The biblical quotations referred to here are "*Seek* and ye shall *find*" and "*Ask* and ye shall *receive*."

414. (B) Think about the order of colors in a rainbow or prism: red, *orange*, *yellow*, green, blue, *indigo*, *violet*.

415. (A) In the life of a star that is not supersized, the order is usually: *protostar, main sequence, red giant, white dwarf*.

416. (B) The numbers 3, 5, 7, and 11 are prime numbers in sequence.

417. (C) All of the characters listed are from plays by Shakespeare. *Cordelia* is one of the daughters of King *Lear*. *Miranda* is the daughter of *Prospero* in *The Tempest*.

418. (B) In the Greek alphabet, *delta* precedes *epsilon* (as D precedes E), and *sigma* precedes *tau* (as S precedes T).

419. (C) The order of steps in the scientific method are typically: ask a *question*, do some research, construct a *hypothesis*, *test* that hypothesis experimentally, do some *analysis* of the data, draw a conclusion, and communicate results.

420. (D) *Delaware* was the first state admitted to the Union, and *Hawaii* was the last. *A* is the first letter of the alphabet, and *Z* is the last.

421. (B) The *Nile* is the longest river in the world, and the *Amazon* is the second longest. *Mount Everest* is the tallest mountain in the world, and *K2* is the second tallest.

422. (A) *Elizabeth I* was the daughter of *Anne Boleyn*. Writer *Mary Shelley* (*Frankenstein*) was the daughter of writer and women's rights advocate *Mary Wollstonecraft*.

423. (A) I *have* is the present tense; I *had* is the past tense. I *am* is the present tense; I *was* is the past tense.

424. (D) *Mr. Bennett* is the father of *Elizabeth* in Jane Austen's *Pride and Prejudice*. *Mr. Cratchit* is the father of Tiny *Tim* in Charles Dickens's *A Christmas Carol*.

425. (A) Something that is *postwar* takes place following *hostilities*. Something that is *posttraumatic* takes place following an *injury*.

426. (B) In a DNA sequence, the purine base *adenine* pairs with the pyrimidine base *thymine*, and the purine base *guanine* pairs with the pyrimidine base *cytosine*.

427. (A) XX = 20, and L = 50. This forms the same ratio as CC (200) to D (500).

428. (D) The *past* is to *yesterday* as the *future* is to *tomorrow*.

429. (A) In geologic time, the *Paleozoic* era precedes the *Mesozoic* era as the *Permian* period precedes the *Triassic* period.

430. (A) In the alphabet, *Y* comes after *X*, and *Q* comes after *P*.

431. (D) In Genesis, *Ishmael* was the son of *Hagar*. In the Shakespearean tragedy that bears his name, *Hamlet* was the son of *Gertrude*.

432. (B) Lyndon *Johnson* was John F. *Kennedy's* vice president and completed his unfinished term of office. Gerald *Ford* was one of Richard *Nixon's* vice presidents and completed his unfinished term of office.

433. (D) A *cub* is a baby *bear*. A *shoat* is a baby *boar*.

434. (A) The prefix *milli-* denotes a number 10 times greater than one with the prefix *micro-*. The same ratio holds for *giga-* and *mega-*.

435. (A) A *triangle* has three sides, a *rectangle* has four sides, a *pentagon* has five sides, and a *hexagon* has six sides.

436. (C) *Advent* is the name of the period of time that leads up to *Christmas*. *Lent* is the name of the period of time that leads up to *Easter*.

437. (A) In the tonic scale, *C* comes just before *D*, and *G* comes just before *A*.

438. (B) The element *hydrogen* has the atomic number 1. *Helium* has the atomic number 2.

439. (C) A *pint* is the equivalent of two *cups*. A *half gallon* is the equivalent of two *quarts*.

440. (C) A *calculator* is the modern or electronic version of an *abacus*, and an *e-book* is the modern or electronic version of a *book*.

441. (B) The fraction 1/32 is half of the fraction 1/16. The fraction 1/8 is half of the fraction 1/4.

442. (C) Just as *alpha* and *omega* are the first and last letters of the Greek alphabet, so *Genesis* and *Revelation* are the first and last books of the Bible.

443. (C) In taxonomy, a *phylum* is a subclass of a *kingdom*, and a *species* is a subclass of a *genus*.

444. (A) In musical notation, *adagio* means "slow," and *andante* means "moderate."

445. (C) *Edward VII's* mother was *Victoria*. *Elizabeth II's* father was *George VI*.

446. (A) Neville *Chamberlain* preceded Winston *Churchill* as prime minister of Great Britain as Margaret *Thatcher* preceded John *Major* several decades later.

447. (B) You *aim* before you *fire*, and you *pour* before you *drink*.

448. (C) A *parr* is a young *salmon*. A *tadpole* is a young *frog*.

449. (C) The *polka* is a Bohemian dance introduced in the *nineteenth* century. The *foxtrot* is an American ballroom dance introduced in the early *twentieth* century.

450. (D) In Roman mythology, *Romulus* and *Remus* were brothers. In Greek mythology, *Hector* and *Paris* were brothers.

Chapter 10: Object/Action Analogies

451. (C) To *defoliate* is to rid of *leaves* in the same way that to *deforest* is to rid of *trees*.

452. (B) *Dizzy Gillespie* was a *trumpet* player in the bebop tradition. *Charlie Parker* was a *saxophone* player in the bebop tradition.

453. (A) These purchases were part of American expansionism. The *Louisiana Purchase* was a transaction with *France*, and the *Gadsden Purchase* was a transaction with *Mexico*.

454. (D) Just as the *liver* produces *bile*, the *kidney* produces *urine*.

455. (A) At a college or university, a *registrar* is usually in charge of student *records*, and a *provost* oversees *curriculum* and instruction.

456. (B) A *plaintiff* may bring a *suit*, but the *court* must determine any *remedy*, or relief, which might include restitution and/or damages.

457. (A) The *Tony* is an award given for achievement in live Broadway musical or drama. The *Booker Prize* is an award given for a British or Irish *novel*.

458. (A) Brain studies indicate that the small part of the brain called the *hypothalamus* is responsible for our *emotions*, whereas the *cerebellum* is responsible for our ability to *balance*.

459. (C) A priest can try to *exorcise*, or remove, an evil *spirit*. A surgeon can try to *excise*, or remove, a *tumor*.

460. (D) A *sprinter* may leap over a *hurdle* in one track-and-field event. In another event, a *pole vaulter* may leap over a *bar*.

461. (D) *Ronald Reagan* appointed *William Rehnquist* to the Supreme Court, and he became chief justice. *John Adams* appointed *John Marshall* to the Supreme Court, where he achieved the same position.

462. (C) The *Thirteenth* Amendment to the Constitution outlawed *slavery*. The *Eighteenth* Amendment to the Constitution outlawed the sale and manufacture of *alcohol*, and the Twenty-first Amendment repealed that amendment.

463. (B) The *Philippine Revolution* signaled the end of *Spain's* rule in the Philippines. The *American Revolution* signaled the end of *England's* rule in the American colonies.

464. (D) One delivers a *eulogy* to *praise* the subject. One writes an *elegy* to *lament* another's passing.

465. (C) An *ophthalmologist* specializes in diseases of the *eyes*. A *periodontist* specializes in diseases of the *gums*.

466. (B) *Unitarianism* is a religion that rejects the notion of the *Trinity*—the oneness of the Father, the Son, and the Holy Ghost. *Anglicanism* is a religion that rejects the *papacy*—the notion that the pope is a conduit between God and humankind.

467. (A) An *ethnologist* might study the *culture* of a region; an *etymologist* might study its *language*.

468. (B) George *Balanchine* was a choreographer and director of the New York City Ballet. Igor *Stravinsky* was a composer who often collaborated with Balanchine.

469. (C) After Robert *Baden-Powell* established the Boy Scouts in the early part of the twentieth century, his sister established the Girl Guides. Juliette Gordon *Low* started a troop in Scotland and then brought the movement home to her native Georgia, changing the name to "Girl Scouts" in 1915.

470. (B) A *farrier* is a blacksmith who works with *iron* and shoes horses. A *furrier* makes or repairs fur (or *hide*) garments.

471. (A) The Greek philosopher *Zeno* founded the Stoic school, which suggested that followers accept all events indifferently as a sign of divine will. The Greek philosopher *Antisthenes* founded the Cynic school, which rejected most of the comforts of society and preached a return to a "natural" life.

472. (C) The *fleur-de-lis* (a kind of iris) is the symbol of *France*. The *lion* is the symbol of *England*.

473. (D) Scottish biologist Alexander *Fleming* discovered *penicillin* in 1928. Edward *Jenner* discovered the *smallpox vaccine* in 1796.

474. (C) A *radiologist* uses *x-rays* in diagnosis and treatment. An *orthotist* designs and uses *braces* and other mechanical devices to correct or support the spine and limbs.

475. (A) *Ovid* wrote the epic poem *Metamorphoses* around the time of the birth of Christ. Franz *Kafka* published his novella *The Metamorphosis* in 1915.

476. (C) A *hertz* is a unit used to measure *frequency*. An *ohm* is a unit used to measure *resistance*.

477. (B) A *tear* is a sign of *sorrow*. A *curtsy* is a sign of *respect*.

478. (A) In the literature of fantasy, a *gremlin* is a creature that perpetrates *mischief*, whereas a *genie* is a creature that grants wishes, or *behests*.

479. (C) George *Eastman* invented roll *film*, once the staple of his company, Eastman Kodak. George *Westinghouse*, who also started a large company bearing his name, invented dozens of electrical devices, cleverly championed AC current despite Thomas Edison's preference for DC, and pioneered the *air brake* for railway trains.

480. (B) A *mason* needs a *trowel* to apply cement. A *woodcarver* needs a *gouge* to cut hollows and curves in wood.

481. (B) A *rash* may be a sign of *rubella* (German measles). *Lockjaw* may be a sign of a *tetanus* infection.

482. (B) *John Boyd Dunlop* invented a *pneumatic tire* in 1888, and Dunlop tires still come from the corporation he founded. *Linus Yale* invented a *cylinder lock* in the 1860s, and Yale locks still come from the corporation he founded.

483. (C) Your *thumb* aids in *grasping* objects. The *arch* of your foot aids in *shock absorption* from the weight of your body against the floor or ground.

484. (D) *Jane Eyre* is the protagonist in a book by Charlotte *Brontë*. Hester Prynne is the protagonist in *The Scarlet Letter* by Nathaniel *Hawthorne*.

485. (C) Your *heart* works to *circulate* blood, and the colorless liquid known as *lymph* works to *defend* against antigens, foreign substances in the body.

486. (C) *Fear* might cause you to *cringe*, or shrink back. *Contempt* might cause you to *sneer*, or turn your nose up.

487. (D) A *burr* is a tool used for *filing* metal. *Shears* are a tool used for *pruning* shrubbery.

488. (C) All of the men listed are virtuoso violinists with the exception of *Yo Yo Ma*, who plays the *cello*.

489. (C) Henry *Hudson* (1565–1611) explored the North American *northeast*. Francisco Vásquez de *Coronado* (1510–1554) explored the American *southwest*.

490. (D) You might *recite* a *poem* aloud, but you would be likely to *expound* (present and explain) a *theory* aloud.

491. (C) An *assessor* reviews information and presents an *evaluation*. A *confessor* hears confessions and provides *absolution* (formal forgiveness).

492. (B) *Lady Chatterley* was a character created by D. H. *Lawrence* in the 1928 novel *Lady Chatterley's Lover*. *Lady Windermere* was a character created by Oscar *Wilde* in the 1892 play *Lady Windermere's Fan*.

493. (C) Scottish explorer/missionary *David Livingstone* led several expeditions to search for the source of the *Nile*. Scottish explorer *Mungo Park* led an expedition to search for the source of the *Niger*.

494. (D) John Maynard *Keynes* is associated with the *new economics*. Norman *Mailer* is associated with the *new journalism*. Neither has been truly "new" for half a century or more.

495. (A) A *judge* interprets and applies the *law*. An *actuary* (a risk-management professional) interprets and applies *probability*.

496. (B) A *bushel* is one unit used to measure dry *volume*. A *fathom* is one unit used to measure liquid *depth*.

497. (A) Samuel *Morse's* key invention, the telegraph, led to progress in the area of *communication*. Edwin *Land's* key invention, instant *photography*, led to progress in the area of photography.

498. (A) The *Nile* empties into the *Mediterranean*. The *Mekong* empties into the *South China Sea*.

499. (C) The *caliber* is a unit used to measure *ammunition* size. The *pica* is a unit used to measure *type* size.

500. (C) A balance *scale* is the symbol of *judgment*. *Seven seals* are a biblical symbol of the *Last Judgment*.